WORLD WAR II
FIGHTERS

JEFFREY L. ETHELL AND ROBERT T. SAND

MBI Publishing Company

This edition published in 2002 by MBI Publishing Company, Galtier Plaza, Suite 200, 380 Jackson Street, St. Paul, MN 55101-3885 USA

MBI Publishing Company books are also available at discounts in bulk quantity for industrial or sales-promotional use. For details write to Special Sales Manager at Motorbooks International Wholesalers & Distributors, Galtier Plaza, Suite 200, 380 Jackson Street, St. Paul, MN 55101-3885 USA.

Library of Congress Cataloging-in-Publication Data Available

ISBN 0-7603-1354-7

On the front cover: On June 2, 1945, less than a month after V-E Day, pilots from the 354th Fighter Squadron, 355th Fighter Group, fly in formation over England. *Alexander C. Sloan via Bob Kuhnert, 355th FG Assn.*

On the frontispiece: Col. Francis "Gabby" Gabreski, 28 aerial victory ace, reveals a common Eighth Air Force fighter pilots' preference—the British leather helmet and oxygen mask. English helmets were more comfortable and afforded better noise protection. The English mask was lined with chamois and had a superior microphone. *USAF/NASM*

On the title page: In mid-1944, the 355th Fighter Group receives a brand-new P-51D at their home base of Steeple Morden, England. *Alexander C. Sloan via Bob Kuhnert, 355th FG Assn.*

On the back cover: The ground crew for Lt. William "Hank" Gruber services *Cooter* at Leiston, England, home of the 357th Fighter Group. *J. E. Frary*

Printed in Hong Kong

Contents

Introduction

By the end of World War II the US Army Air Forces stretched across the globe with a seemingly endless supply of aircraft, aircrew and ground crew. American industrial might and military training, in a few short years, had geared up from lethargy to a frenzy of mass production. Seldom are the sheer numbers ever mentioned, and even then they are so large as to be incomprehensible.

From 1 July 1940 to 30 August 1945 the United States manufactured 299,293 aircraft. Of those, 69,118 were for the US Navy and in the massive Lend-Lease effort to supply the Allies, over 43,000 aircraft were sent to the Soviet Union and Great Britain. By comparison, the United Kingdom built 128,835 aircraft from 1939 to 1945, Germany rolled out 113,514 (53,728 of which were fighters) and Japan produced 58,834 from 1941 to 1945.

As astonishing as it seems today, 9,535 P-38s were built at an average cost of $97,147 each; 15,579 P-47s for $85,578 apiece; 14,490 P-51s for $51,572 each; 12,677 B-17s for $204,370 each; 18,188 B-24s for $215,516 per copy; and on the list goes.

To man these aircraft the USAAF trained 193,440 pilots and washed out another 124,000 from 1 July 1939 to 31 August 1945 while training over 400,000 aircrew to man the bombers and transports with bombardiers, navigators, gunners, flight engineers and other specialists. To support every one man in combat, the AAF had to field sixteen noncombat personnel. There were seven ground crew for every man who flew and four ground technical specialists for every one man in the air.

How well were these men paid? In 1944 a private got $50 a month, a staff sergeant $96, a master sergeant $138. Yearly pay for a second lieutenant was $1,800, a major got $3,000, a bird colonel $4,000 and a four-star general $8,000.

By June 1944 here's what it cost to outfit the average fighter pilot: gloves $1.74, goggles $10.74, sun glasses $3.25, helmet $1.16, A-2 jacket $8.12, winter flying jacket $25.00, summer flying suit $8.50 and Mae West $10.00.

There never was, and there never will be, another flying armada to equal the wartime US Army Air Forces.

From this war machine emerged but 35,000 fighter pilots supported by highly competent and technically savvy ground crews.

As much as it made their fellow bomber pilots furious, fighter pilots were the glamor boys of the "Air Corps"—in spite of a name change to AAF in 1941, the older, more romantic term stuck throughout the war, even in official documents and reports. The dashing fighter pilot in his leather jacket, fifty-mission "crush" hat and silk scarf was idolized by the press and chased by the girls. But when a bomber was in serious trouble, the feisty "Little Friend" was a savior . . . fighter pilots were welcome at bars or pubs and told they could not pay for a single drink. There isn't a bomber crewman alive who didn't heave a massive sigh of relief at the sight of a Lightning, Thunderbolt or Mustang over enemy territory.

Certainly the AAF had a tough time dealing with these aggressive men who flew single-seat aircraft, relying on themselves and their skill—"you can always tell a fighter pilot, but you can't tell him much." By his very nature, a fighter pilot had to believe that he was the best at what he did, that no one else could fly a plane like he could, that the enemy was going to die in a dogfight, that the other guy was going to "auger in" and kill himself through some stupid mistake.

Otherwise, he would never have gone to war alone at 30,000 feet, deep in enemy territory, looking for enemy aircraft to shoot down or flak-infested airdromes to shoot up. The pilot who loved flying single-seat aircraft with no crew to rely on was often the one who tore apart the local base officer's club for a good time or threw the commanding general in the pool. The exceptional wartime fighter pilot had little patience with peacetime flying and the social climbing required for promotion.

In the background sat the hard-working ground crew. Though they never got the glory, they basked in the satisfaction of giving their pilots the best maintenance possible. A kill was earned by the whole team but when "their" airplane came back all shot up, the crew chief and his men would listen impatiently while the pilot had some tall explaining to do.

Beneath all the banter and the caste system which kept officer and enlisted man apart, the Army fighter outfits were the epitome of teamwork, both on the ground and in the air. The fighter was, for the most part, overshadowed by prewar faith in the ability of the strategic bomber to survive enemy attack. Until the escort fighter arrived, bombers were hacked down in ever-increasing numbers. Nowhere was this more evident than in the European Theater of Operations (ETO) when, by the end of 1943, the Eighth Air Force bomber offensive was close to being stopped by the Luftwaffe.

Though the Republic P-47 Thunderbolt had been covering the bombers through most of 1943, its lack of range left the "Big Friends" alone deep in enemy territory. With the arrival of the Lockheed P-38 Lightning in late 1943, then the North American P-51 Mustang in early 1944, the fortunes of war changed as Eighth AF commanding general Jimmy Doolittle turned his fighter pilots loose under the command of Gen. Bill Kepner. No longer restricted to escorting within visual range of the bombers, fighter pilots roamed Germany at altitude and on the deck to destroy the Luftwaffe and the Wehrmacht; from that point, the outcome of the airwar was a foregone conclusion. The tactical fighter units of Gen. Pete Quesada's Ninth Air Force came into their own as they supported the ground forces deep into Germany, strafing and bombing everything in sight.

In the Mediterranean Theater of Operations (MTO) American fighter pilots were thrown into the meat grinder of North Africa at the end of 1942 to face an experienced enemy. The campaign moved slowly up to Sicily and Italy as the "soft underbelly of Europe" proved to be anything but. Fighter groups of the Twelfth and Fifteenth Air Forces provided escort deep into Germany from the south and then went after targets on the ground under the leadership of Generals Ira Eaker and Nate Twining.

Though the exploits of these fighter pilots and their crews are well known, they are set in a sepia-toned memory for later generations. The first batches of experimental color film from Kodak were hard to find, leaving photographers with little choice but to record events in black and white. This book will change that memory and give the reader the first full-blown exposure to outstanding color photography of pilots and ground crews as they lived their lives, accompanied by the vivid narration of first-person recollection.

A fortunate few managed to scrounge up some rolls of Kodachrome and record what was going on around them, among them the coauthor of this book, Bob Sand. Many of the photos are his, and they come to life with his recollections written at the time in a diary and in letters home, which his parents saved. Bob had one continual request—send more Kodachrome when it could be found.

Like most enlisted ground crew, Bob led what he considers to be an unspectacular life in the propeller shop, then as a member of a P-51 ground crew, in the 55th Fighter Group, first at Nuthampstead, then at Wormingford, England. Just after his arrival in England, he wrote his parents on Thanksgiving 1943, "I've shot up one roll of [Kodachrome] film, and while this roll contains nothing spectacular, I hope it is the beginning of something that may have a little interest later on. I'm a little worried about light conditions. I only shoot when sun is bright." No wonder—the film had an ASA of around 12!

That was the beginning. Bob's uncanny eye for using a camera often led to him being ridiculed for carrying the thing around all the time. Fortunately, for those of us who were born later, he did not let that stop him. The result is, without question, some of the finest wartime photography in existence. In many ways this book is his lasting testament to life in a fighter group during World War II.

The narrative portions of the 55th Group in the air, written by former pilot Arthur L. Thorsen, are vibrantly alive, adding yet another dimension to Bob's photos. Thanks to Gen. Regis Urschler for sending a copy of Art's unpublished manuscript, "The Fighting 55th." With Art's kind permission we have been

7

able to let the reader fly along with him and live the life of a fighter pilot.

Other unpublished memoirs were provided by 339th Fighter Group pilot James R. Hanson, who chronicled his career in the AAF, through Korea to his days flying for Piedmont Airlines, and Gilbert C. Burns, Jr., a 50th Fighter Group pilot who was in the thick of Ninth Air Force ground support activity. Without question the Thorsen, Hanson and Burns manuscripts deserve to be published; they put the reader straight back into the emotion of those times. Should a publisher reading this book be sufficiently impressed with what they read from these men, we would welcome an inquiry to put the parties together.

Had it not been for the 55th Fighter Group Association editor Chet Patterson, none of this would have been possible. After seeing a video tape of his presentation using Bob's slides, I prevailed upon him to put me in touch with Bob and this project was born. He then sent several excellent editions of the 55th newsletter, along with his own recollections, thus rounding out our look at the group in wartime England.

Once the project got under way, we attempted to broaden its scope and made a series of requests to people who had taken color slides during the war. With typical generosity, many responded.

The exceptional understanding of Duane J. Reed, curator of special collections in the US Air Force Academy Library, will long be remembered. He provided access to the outstanding Mark H. Brown photography collection, and his assistant, Robert Troudt, was always willing to help us find what we needed. John Woolnough, editor of the *Eighth Air Force News,* sent his collection of wartime color slides which had come from a number of veterans. That opened more doors in finding 357th Fighter Group veteran Jim Frary and 386th Bomb Group pilot Byron Trent, both of whom sent their precious original slides.

As usual, Bob Kuhnert of the 355th FG Assn. came through in his usual selfless fashion and copied Alexander C. "Cal" Sloan's fabulous slide collection, as well as sending several of his favorite issues of *Mustang,* the group newsletter which he so ably edits, and some of his own recollections. Cal was attached to the 1066th Signal Company at Steeple Morden with the 355th. He kept his camera with him as well.

Through the generosity of the 4th FG Assn.'s Charles E. Konsler, we found 4th Fighter Group veterans Edward B. Richie, Joseph B. Sills and Donald E. Allen. Ed, along with sons Mark and Alan, reloaned Ed's fantastic collection of wartime slides, as did Joe and Don.

Through the friendship of P–51 owner Joe Scogna we were put in contact with 356th Fighter Group pilot Herbert R. Rutland, Jr., who took his camera along with him over Germany in the cockpit of his Mustang for some of the most stunning combat color photography to come out of the war, as well as some poignant memories of leaving the fighter pilot's life at the end of the war. Jack and Jan (Houston) Monaghan jumped in with relish to tell of their days in the 55th Fighter Group from the enlisted man's side and through the eyes of a Red Cross girl in a world of men.

Richard H. Perley, and Philip Savides sent slides of their Ninth Air Force, 50th Fighter Group tours of duty, while Gil Burns passed on some of Phil's wartime recollections. Another Ninth Air Force pilot, Arthur O. Houston of the 368th Fighter Group, provided exceptional slides, as he has always has.

Thanks to the willingness of 14th Fighter Group ground crewman Ira Latour and 31st Fighter Group pilot William J. Skinner, the book was able to branch out into coverage of North Africa and the MTO through the many slides they took during their time overseas. Many thanks to Chris Davis for introducing us to William Skinner. Through leading fighter historian Steve Blake, these were added to by Walter E. Zurney who flew with the 82nd Fighter Group and managed to get a roll of Kodachrome in the process.

In searching out recollections from people who had served in fighter units, we found several to be more than willing to jump in. Eric V. Hawkinson, editor of the 7th Photo Group Journal, sent numerous issues with great stories of the unheralded job of recon flying and George Lawson, former 7th Photographic Reconnaissance Group commander and president of the Eighth Air Force Historical Society, put his support behind the project as well. The irrepressible Jack Ilfrey (USAAF class of '41 with my dad, Erv Ethell) opened the 20th Fighter Group archives to send the late John Hudgens' color shots while Leo D. Lester of the 56th Fighter Group Association and Robert H. Powell, Jr., of the 352nd Fighter Group Association interrupted their own association projects to help. Thanks, also, to James Starnes of the 339th Fighter Group Association for history and photos.

Fellow historians Roger Freeman, David Menard, Larry Davis, Samuel Sox, Tom Hitchcock of Monogram Aviation Publications, Bill Hess, Pete Bowers, Dana Bell and Robert DeGroat supplied rare material from their archives while Melissa Kaiser, Dan Hagedorn, Larry Wilson and Mark Avino helped me gain continual access to the National Air & Space Museum (NASM) USAAF color collection.

Then there were the vets themselves who recalled those unforgettable days: William B. Bailey, Duane W. Beeson, Arthur O. Beimdiek, William Bell, Donald J.M. Blakeslee, Marvin Bledsoe, Wayne K. Blickenstaff, John Blyth, Henry W. Brown, Dan Burrows, Thomas J.J. Christian, Jr., Harry Corey, Harry J. Dayhuff, James H. Doolittle, Ervin C. Ethell, Edward B. Giller, Herman Greiner, Walter Hagenah, John B. Henry, Jr., Mark E. Hubbard, Stanley A. Hutchins, Norman W. Jackson, Herbert E. Johnson, Robert S. Johnson, Thomas H. Jones, Claiborne H. Kinnard, Jr., Heinz Knoke, Jean Landis, Don Larson, Jack Lenox, Daniel M. Lewis, Walker M. Mahurin, Chester Marshall, Joe L. Mason, V. K. Meroney, John C. Meyer, Erwin Miller, John Most, John B. Murphy, Elmer W. O'Dell, Ben Rimerman, Robb Satterfield, David C. Schilling, Frank C. Shearin, Jr., Ernst Schroeder, Robert Shoens, Bert Stiles, Avelin P. Tacon, Jr., Harrison B. Tordoff, Ralph P. Willett, Paul Wingert and Hubert Zemke.

The Eighth Air Force tactics manuals, *The Long Reach* and *Down to Earth*, put together by VIII Fighter Command Generals Bill Kepner and Francis Griswold in 1944, added a great deal to placing the reader straight into those times with on-the-spot recollections of serving fighter pilots who described the events as they took place.

For keeping Bob supplied with Kodachrome we would like to thank his parents, Oscar and Rosa Sand, and his friends Violet and Archie Gerry.

For encouragement, we thank George Cockle, McCauley Clark and Danny Morris.

For retyping a massive portion of the manuscript for her dad, we thank Jennie Ethell.

We particularly want to thank our wives, Bettie Ethell and Donna Sand, for their unwavering support.

To all of you, we express our warmest thanks for making the days of Fighter Command come alive again.

Jeff Ethell,
Bob Sand

Chapter 1

So You Want to Be a Fighter Pilot?

William Bell, *AT-6 flying cadet*

Once we got into advanced training with a hot 600 hp airplane, we flying cadets considered it the hot rod we never could afford during the Depression. We would cruise about the Texas plains after dark, harassing train crewmen to the point of serious injury. We would spot a slow freighter ambling along a track, fly ahead of it for several miles, turn and meet the locomotive at cab level, and wait until we were right on the engine before turning on one landing light. The engineer would *know* that he couldn't stop in time to avoid a *sure* collision, and order the fireman to jump before the "other train" hit. The engineer

A fighter! During the last few hours of advanced training a select few Cadets were allowed to log their last solo time in an older model pursuit ship. Others who went on to fighter transition had to wait until graduation and getting wings. This obsolete Curtiss P–40B was flown from Luke Field, Arizona, in 1942. That it had seen better days was irrelevant to a pilot moving up from an AT-6. *USAF*

Stateside Mustang transition appears to agree with these fledgling fighter pilots, fresh out of advanced training in late 1943. The AT–6 and A–20 in the background form part of the base's complement of aircraft as well. Judging from the exhaust trail on the P–51A, the fighters were ridden hard and put away wet. *USAF*

promptly slammed on the brakes and ground the wheels flat as the AT-6 roared overhead and we hightailed it back to base with our night flying training completed. This was great sport for both Army and Navy pilots.

John Most, *AT-6 flying cadet*

As students we'd play a game during formation flying—the wingman had to get his wingtip as close as possible to the leader's fuselage . . . between his wing and his tail . . . and not hit him.

Robb Satterfield, *AT-6 flying cadet*

For all local flying we had a tower officer, usually a first lieutenant, to handle emergencies and back up the enlisted tower personnel. One day this boy captain was tower officer, a recent overseas returnee with many ribbons and fairly well impressed with himself. Suddenly, over the radio comes the message, 'King Uncle, King Uncle (Williams Tower)! This is Yoke Three Four! My engine just quit! What shall I do?' Our captain hero wades through the sergeants and corporals, grabs the mike, and says, 'Yoke Three Four, this is *Captain* Snodgrass [meaning your troubles are all over, I'm here]. Stay calm, mister. What is your position?' The cadet came back, 'King Uncle, this is Yoke Three Four. I'm still on the ramp. I haven't taxied out yet.' At this, our captain turns instant red and tried to melt into the floor. He was a rather subdued fellow—for maybe three days.

Robb Satterfield, *AT-6 pilot*

I was on the morning schedule as a recently commissioned pilot, which meant from about 0600 till noon on the flight line. Just at noon a beautiful brand new P-51D, first bubble '51 any of us had seen, came over the field at about 1,500 feet, did a roll, entered the pattern, landed and parked at base ops about 150 yards away. As the super fighter enthusiast in the gang, I grabbed up about four or five friends and we headed down to ops to see the Mustang. As we got within about 100 feet of the bird, the pilot, in summer flying suit, stepped out on the wing, took off the helmet and shook out *her* long blond curls! That did it. We halted in our tracks, spun on our heels and strode back to squadron ops,

Barbara Jane Erickson (in the cockpit) is congratulated by Evelyn Sharp, 6th Ferry Group, Women's Auxiliary Ferrying Squadron (WAFS) after delivering a P-51A to Long Beach, California, in early 1943. Much to the consternation of many male fighter pilots, as the war went on the number of women pilots grew until the Women Airforce Service Pilots (WASPs) were formed in July 1943. Sharp was later killed in the crash of a P-38, while Erickson survived the war to win an Air Medal for her outstanding ferry service. *USAF*

The AT-6 was the first dose of real horsepower given to Army Air Force Cadets and they took to the beefy trainer with unbridled enthusiasm, much to the horror of local townspeople who were constantly buzzed and chased at all hours of the day and night. It was intoxicating to ride behind 600 horsepower with the canopy slid back and the landing gear tucked up. A pilot's first taste of "rat racing" in trail, leader trying to shake those following, came with the Texan. *USAF*

five very unhappy 19 to 22 year old 2nd lieutenants.

Jean Landis, *Women's Airforce Service Pilot*

Reactions to a woman climbing out of a P-51 were varied, mostly startled. Once I flew into a field that was off limits but the weather was bad and I had a slight mechanical problem so I called in and asked for permission to land. I kept radioing, "P-51 ready to land; awaiting final landing instructions." It was sort of garbled and they kept asking me to call in again and again. Finally, they said, "Waggle your wings if you receive." Then, "Lady, the only thing we see up there is a P-51." They couldn't believe it—they were looking for a Piper Cub or something. Finally, when I landed, what a welcome I got. Word got around that a gal was flying that thing. They were darlings. By the time

Airacobra training at Hamilton Field, California, for the 357th Fighter Group before shipping out to England to join the Eighth Air Force in July 1943. Group CO Col. Edward S. Chickering's P-39 is being started by the ground crew the hard way—with the hand crank to get the inertia starter going. *NASM*

I had taxied up to the line, following the little Follow Me truck, there were lots of guys around to see what kind of woman was flying this P-51. They'd never heard of us, the WASPs. **James R. Hanson,** *fighter transition*

My first flight in the 'Cobra is tremendous. I'm all strapped in and the crew chief gives me the clear signal. When I press my heel to the starter, there's a squeal, then a couple cylinders bark and with a few shakes from nose to tail the 12 cylinder Allison comes to life with a roar. You can feel the fuselage twist as the long driveshaft takes up the torque. My instructor gives me the thumbs up and waves me out.

As I roll into position I really appreciate the forward visibility and advance the throttle. The take-off is a real joy . . . a simple flip of the toggle switch brings the gear up. I was prepared for the solid feel of a fighter

Army Air Corps pilots dreamed of flying the hot ships after getting out of advanced training. When a new Lightning like this one would show up and dazzle the Flying Cadets, there would be a rush for the few fighter slots available. This hot rock shows real fighter pilot savoir-faire for the troops (more likely the photographer) by stepping into his '38 with the engines running. *NASM*

14

this time, having been one of the lucky ones to have flown the P-40 for six hours. Except for the solid feel, everything else is different. In the P-40 the whole airplane seems to spread out ahead of you since you sit behind the long nose and back over the trailing edge of the wing. Here in the '39, sitting high over the leading edge, I feel like the wings are strapped onto my hips. The climb is better and the controls are lighter. It's everything I've dreamed about. There are some scattered clouds up here to play with and then I do some steep turns, a roll, and pull vapors off the wingtips.

Frank C. Shearin, Jr., *P-38 pilot, fighter transition*

During the course of four ship P-38 student navigation flight (one instructor and three students), positions were changed to where I was leading the second element with a student on my wing. It was a beautiful day and the sun made the cockpit cozy. After approximately 20 minutes, I noticed my wingman slowly leave the formation up and to the right. Over the radio I yelled, "Bartlett!" The wings of his aircraft fluttered and he returned to the formation. Shortly thereafter he left the formation again—slowly up and to the right. Again I yelled, "Bartlett!" with the same reaction. His wings fluttered and he returned to the formation. Upon landing I asked him why he left the formation. He replied, "The sun made me sleepy, so I trimmed the aircraft to fly up and to the right in case I fell asleep. I didn't want to fall asleep and run into you."

Ervin C. Ethell, *P-63 pilot and gunnery instructor*

During the maneuvers in the California desert while serving as a practice antiaircraft target, I decided to show the ground pounders how us Army pilots could fly. Roaring over the makeshift airfield adjacent to the bivouac, I came in on the deck, pulled the nose up and started a slow roll. As I got upside down the nose fell through—I wasn't going to make it. Shoving with all my might, both feet on one rudder and both hands on the stick, I got the P-63 reversed in what must have been a reverse snap roll but she was shuddering on the edge of a stall as I pulled back on the stick. I just missed the commanding general's tent but proceeded to blow it down on top of him with my considerable prop wash. Sand, tumbleweeds and who knows what else formed a wake behind me as I tried to keep from mushing in, hovering in ground effect—for some unknown reason the fighter stayed airborne, slowly regaining flying speed.

I calmed down enough to quit shaking and headed back for Muroc, knowing I was going to get court martialed for sure. After landing I took a look under my airplane, sure the belly must have dragged the desert, miraculously missing the prop. No damage but I had to pick quite a few tumbleweeds out of the small air scoop on the belly. The worst was yet to come—as was usual after a sortie, I had to take the Jeep and drive out to the general's tent for a debrief on the day's results. When I arrived his first words to me were, "You blew my tent down!" Bracing for the chewing out, I saw him break into a wide grin and

say, "Can you come back tomorrow and do that great show again?"

Thomas E. Maloney, *P-38 pilot, fighter transition*

I'll never forget my P-38 instructor, Capt. Erv Ethell, a North Africa combat veteran. After he briefed us on the mission for the day, we would get in a jeep or command car and he would have us each dropped off at our planes. He would be the last to get to his. No matter how fast you would climb up, get in your chute and crank that old bird up, when we got the engines started and taxied out, he would always be out at the head of the taxi strip waiting on us. Naturally, this got to be quite a game we played but by the end of our three weeks training he would still beat us out just as badly as at first. I naturally got very proficient at this with continued practice and as the P-38 got to be a part of me, but in my best days, I'm sure Captain Ethell would still be out on the end of the runway waiting for me since we later found out he contorted his arms, hands and fingers in such a way that he could start both engines at once. Us hot rock, brand new shavetail fighter pilots found out we had some things to learn.

Andy Anderson, *AT-6 student*

I was once privileged to see one of the Chinese trainees land his Curtiss P-40 on the taxiway adjacent to the parking area. Somehow he became disoriented and put it down, just as a weaving class of AT-6s was working their way into the parking areas. There must have been five or six AT-6s S-ing when the P-40 touched down coming at them head-on, at about ninety miles per hour. I

15

was told later that the tower operators were going out of their collective minds trying to get the Chinese fighter pilot to go around, this before he touched down. Story has it that he kept responding to their instructions by replying, 'Loger, loger, loger.' In any event, the AT-6s—all of them saw him coming and either dived into the parking area or plunged out onto the mat to let him get by. He managed to get it stopped and all those cadets in the AT-6s survived without a dented wingtip.

Pete Vandersluis, *AT-6 instructor*
    The first student I had got on the wobble pump and the primer, then

Who cares if this is a staged AAF public relations shot? No question this Flying Cadet at Luke Field, Arizona, 1941, is happy to climb into the hot rod he could never afford during the depression. Only *this* one has wings and 600 hp under the hood. *USAF*

A fighter transition P–39D Airacobra on the line at Page Field, Ft. Myers, Florida in March 1943. *William J. Skinner*

The expression says it all ... Though the P–39 was not greatly loved by most who flew it in combat, when it was the first fighter given to a new shavetail second looie out of Advanced, it was "hawg heaven." This instructor at Ft. Myers, Florida seems to mirror his students' enthusiasm—or relish what he is about to introduce them to. *William J. Skinner*

backfired the engine which caught fire. Every time he would hit the primer and the wobble pump, the flames went higher around the cowl and I was yelling at him to stop priming. I opened the throttle and tried to pull the mixture to idle cut-off. Of course with the lock on the mixture in the front cockpit, I couldn't do it and I'm yelling at him to pull the mixture to idle cut-off. The flames really started spreading, so about then I yelled, "Get out!," turned off everything, threw my shoulder harness and seat belt off, left my chute on and jumped out. As I jumped up on the step, the shoulder harness caught in my parachute and my foot came off the step. I came down on the canopy rail you know where, went headfirst over and hung with my head about a foot from the ground, upside down by my shoulder harness.

It wasn't more than a few seconds, before I was covered with foam from head to toe from the fire truck. That was my first check ride. The student was so rattled he failed and washed out.

James R. Hanson, *BT-13 student*

Just below I saw a BT do a slow roll—when it got inverted someone fell out. I heard the student yell over the radio. "My instructor fell out, my instructor fell out!" The plane scooped out but the cadet was really shook up. I told him to just fly the plane and go back to the field, then I dropped down and watched the instructor come

down in his chute and land in the trees. I radioed his position. When we got to him after his recovery we found that he got a cut lip and a lot of razzing from his fellow instructors.

Chester Marshall, *PT-19 student* (*from his book* Sky Giants Over Japan *by Chester Marshall, Apollo Books, 1984)*

Then came the slow roll. By this time I was concentrating deeply on the movements and instruments and I failed to realize that strange things were beginning to happen in my cockpit. That is, until we started into inverted flight. First, there was a floating sensation. I surmised that was associated with the slow roll feeling. But as the maneuver progressed, I departed farther from my seat. By the time the plane was upside down I was flapping in the breeze *outside the cockpit,* or at least 99% of my body was. Luckily, during my abrupt departure, I locked the toes of my right foot under the top edge of the cockpit and tightened my one-hand death grip on the stick.

Slip stream and gravitation came close to winning the struggle, but the instructor somehow overpowered my deadweight grip on the stick and flipped the plane upright. Embarrassed, I plopped into the cockpit, headfirst.

After verifying that all was well, the instructor broke into uproarious laughter, muttering something about the funniest sight he had ever seen,

and he bellowed over the tube: "I'll bet you never forget to fasten your safety belt again." He was right. I didn't.

Charles A. Lindbergh, *P-38 pilot, 475th Fighter Group*

Science, freedom, beauty, adventure: what more could you ask of life? Aviation combined all the elements I loved. There was science in each curve of an airfoil, in each angle between strut and wire, in the gap of a spark plug or the color of the exhaust flame. There was freedom in the unlimited horizon, on the open fields where one landed. A pilot was surrounded by beauty of earth and sky. He brushed treetops with the birds, leapt valleys and rivers, explored the cloud canyons he had gazed at as a child. Adventure lay in each puff of wind.

I began to feel that I lived on a higher plane than the skeptics on the ground—one that was richer because of its very association with the element of danger they dreaded, because it was freeer of the earth to which they were bound. In flying, I tasted a wine of the gods of which they could know nothing. Who valued life more highly, the aviators who spent it on the art they loved, or these misers who doled it out like pennies through their antlike days? I decided that if I could fly for ten years before I was killed in a crash, it would be a worthwhile trade for an ordinary lifetime.

Chapter 2

Mud, Sand, and Sweat:
North Africa and the MTO

Ervin C. Ethell, *P-38 pilot, 14th Fighter Group*

During a sweep near Tunis we discovered, after turning around for Maison Blanche, we had overextended our range so we'd have to land and refuel. It was late in the evening and as nightfall settled, we received a vector from the British to land at Bone, a field manned by the now friendly French with no runway lights. Open five gallon cans were half filled with dirt and soaked with gasoline. When lit they gave a reasonably good outline of the landing strip.

As each P-38 landed the pilot was signaled to brake, get out and leave his aircraft unmoved until

Three 308th Fighter Squadron officers ponder the L-shaped slit trench they have just excavated from the North African hard pan. The trench had not existed the previous night when the unit experienced its first German air raid on the field at Korba, near Cape Bon, Tunisia. Left to right are "Dutchy" Holland, Dick Hurd and Don Walker. The three men had it finished before sundown. *William J. Skinner*

The 14th Fighter Group's North African bases during 1942 were barren stretches of Tunisian desert. Pilots and ground crews lived in tents or holes and food was the major topic of conversation. *Ira Latour*

18

daylight. After getting out of my ship, *Tangerine,* I walked to the rear instead of the nose as I usually did. The next morning I found my nosewheel less than three feet from the edge of a 200 foot cliff overlooking the sea.

Arthur O. Beimdiek, *P-38 pilot, 14th Fighter Group*

In North Africa if the supply people got the mail through, they had done a good job, even if the food and ammunition didn't make it. At the forward bases, they flew almost everything in with C-47s. These pilots told us the lead C-47 carried the mail; the rest of our supplies came in the others. The lead plane with the mail landed first. If he made it safely on our

An RAF air-sea rescue Walrus sits ready at Korba, Cape Bon, Tunisia. These lumbering biplanes were a most welcome sight across Europe and the Mediterranean when a downed flier was sitting in a raft or bobbing in his Mae West. Tragically, the pilot of this aircraft was killed during the first German air raid on Korba in May 1943, leaving the American 31st Fighter Group without rescue support until another pilot was transferred in. *William J. Skinner*

American fighter pilots in the Mediterranean had a fantastic form of recreation very seldom matched in other theaters of war—flying captured enemy aircraft. Occupying one enemy airfield after another, units would find numerous enemy aircraft left behind. This Me 109 was reworked by 31st Fighter Group mechanics in their spare time, put back in airworthy shape and flown by the pilots to compare performance. The 109 was painted overall sand yellow in order to make it conspicuous when in the air; no one wanted to get shot down while hot rodding in the Messerschmitt. *William J. Skinner*

Americans were in for some colorful culture changes overseas. When Bill Skinner arrived in North Africa he met this friendly water vendor on the streets of Casablanca, Morocco, complete with goatskin bladder and drinking cups. *William J. Skinner*

19

usually muddy field, the rest would come in. If not, at least we got our mail.

Thomas H. Jones, *P-38 pilot, 82nd Fighter Group*

I'll never forget my first combat field in North Africa and the surrounding area—looked like something out of *Grapes of Wrath.* Wash hanging on lines and tent roofs—chickens tied with string to tent ropes and eggs lying in the helmet liners by the tent doors—all belonging to P-38 jocks who had done some trading with the "Arabs," as North African natives were labeled. Chickens and eggs for mattress covers, which the Arabs prized, cut arm holes in and wore.

William J. Skinner, *Spitfire pilot, 31st Fighter Group*

At Pomigliano we were assigned some beautiful four-story-high apartments formerly used by Italian factory workers. When the Germans would come over at night to bomb Naples, which they did with monotonous regularity, they came right over the apartments. Mt. Vesuvius was right behind us, which was always lit up, so the bombers would pass over the volcano, make a turn of so many degrees, wait so many seconds, then drop their bombs. Naples couldn't get out of the way, and the Germans were bound to hit something.

Another 31st Fighter Group recreational vehicle—*Wacky Macchi,* a captured Italian Macchi C.202 Folgore. The Macchi was the equal of any fighter in the theater. Unfortunately, it didn't fly for long due to lack of compatible hydraulic fluid and no spare tires. *William J. Skinner*

Though it was unusual for Spitfire pilots to see a heavy bomber up close, B–24D *Bathtub Bessie* made an unscheduled landing at the 308th Fighter Squadron's base in North Africa while trying to get back to base, 1943. *William J. Skinner*

Termini, Imerese Airfield, the 31st Fighter Group's base on the north coast of Sicily . . . as Bill Skinner remembered, "Leetle mud in Sicily. Knothaid tried to go through." A Dodge command car, which seemed to be able to go through anything, comes to the rescue and pulls a jeep from the thick, slimy, sucking slough. *William J. Skinner*

Flak was going up all over . . . we'd go up on the roof and watch . . . it was like the 4th of July. Every once in awhile night fighters would go up there—we'd see tracers going back, tracers going up. Once we heard a bomber wind up and go down with a big boom. A big cheer! Later we found out it was an A-20, which was no plane to be night fighting in. We didn't know if he was hit or got vertigo.

Norman W. Jackson, *P-38 pilot, 14th Fighter Group*

By the time I had 30 hours of combat, I had bailed out, crash landed in the desert, come home on one engine and brought one more home so

Bob Hope and his main morale booster, Frances Langford, giving it their best at Palermo, Sicily, 1943, for members of the 31st Fighter Group. *William J. Skinner*

August 1943, Cape Milazzo, Sicily. A 308th Fighter Squadron Spitfire Mk. VIII with a 90 gallon auxiliary fuel tank sits in front of a doctor's vineyard villa. Flying missions from such a sylvan setting pointed up the incongruity of war, but no one thought about it much. Quarters such as these were a break from tents and barren open stretches. *William J. Skinner*

Cape Milazzo, Sicily, September 1943. Bill Skinner dejectedly looks over his first Spitfire Mk. VB, now broken and bent beyond repair. The 308th Fighter Squadron had moved up to this forward area field to cover the invasion of Italy. The dry dust kicked up through the Marston mat pierced steel planking became a nightmare. Taxiing through the choking dust, Bill stopped to clear the area ahead but wingman Ed Fardella behind couldn't see a thing and ran his Spit right up the back of his leader. Unfortunately Ed's fighter was equipped with a metal rather than a wood prop. Instead of breaking apart it proceeded to chop the tail, then dig in just behind the cockpit. Fardella's spinner was almost in Skinner's cockpit when he realized what was happening and cut the engine. *William J. Skinner*

shot up that it was junked. There was talk of presenting me with the German Iron Cross.

William J. Skinner, *Spitfire pilot, 31st Fighter Group*

Our Spitfires and the P-51Bs that replaced them had the same Rolls-Royce Merlin engine, but the P-51 had a laminar flow wing which gave it 10 mph more speed straight and level and much greater fire power with .50 caliber machine guns. When strafing a target with the Mustang it seemed like I'd never run out of ammunition while the Spit had 120 rounds each for the two cannon and 350 for each .303, which was a good gun but didn't have much power. But the Spit had excellent maneuverability and rate of climb and no restrictions on maneuvers performed. The British never gave us any flight manuals, just word of mouth. We'd ask these guys what we could or couldn't do and they'd say, "Hell, you've got a fighter plane; you can do anything you want . . . straight down, full throttle . . . put your feet on the upper rudder pedals and pull back as hard as you can.

Bill Skinner takes a pensive look at his Spitfire Mk. V after returning to the 31st Fighter Group base at Montecorvino, Italy on 1 October 1943 after covering the landings at Salerno. An 88 mm flak shell went off between him and his wingman, putting a sizeable dent in his Spit. *William J. Skinner*

Nothing's going to happen." You couldn't do that with many other planes.

However the Spit was short ranged, even with the 90 gallon auxiliary belly tank. It was good for escorting A-20s, B-25s, B-26s, but we didn't have the range to escort the heavy bombers, and that's where the '51 came in.

For the average fighter pilot, if you got in trouble, you were better off in the Spit than the '51. Your chances of surviving were better because you could maneuver out of tight spots. I got in a situation where I was tangling with six Me 109s and I didn't get a bullet hole in the plane. Four I could keep track of . . . they bounced us when I was flying on a friend's wing.

My radio was out and I kept trying to tell him these guys were coming in . . . I just couldn't wait any longer so I broke into them. We went head-on for several passes and I got a couple of hits on one of them but it didn't seem to bother him too much. We finally broke it off. I wasn't too happy but I didn't feel as uncomfortable as I would have in a '51.

308th Fighter Squadron pilots wait in front of their mess hall in the early morning sunlight for the truck to take them back to their field at Pomigliano, Italy. The building used to house the local workers' nursery before the Allied invasion. *William J. Skinner*

The Spitfire was a fun plane to fly—there was nothing to worry about. It looked nice, it felt nice, it flew nice—it didn't take very long before you felt very comfortable in it. The narrow landing gear didn't seem to make any difference on landing—the AT-6 was much worse. The Spit had no tendency to ground loop.

The pilots in my squadron weren't too happy about giving up their Spits for '51s. They were used to the Spit and knew what it would do while the Mustang was sort of an unknown thing. Unfortunately the 31st Group had to build up P-51 time on missions without any real transition . . . that's not really the place to learn your limitations. But they were looking forward to the '51 in another way because it had the range . . . after

A 308th Fighter Squadron Spitfire Mk. VB at sunset looking toward Mt. Vesuvius at Pomigliano, Italy. Though the deep chin dust filter under the spinner kept engines healthy, it cut performance significantly. *William J. Skinner*

25

all, we were fighter pilots and we wanted to get into a fight. Flying patrol so much and never getting into a dogfight could get pretty old . . . the '51 assured you were going to run into something on almost every mission. You had a well-built plane, good firepower, the range and if you kept your head up and didn't let the Germans get behind you, your chances of surviving were pretty good.

Arthur O. Beimdiek, *P-38 pilot, 14th Fighter Group*
Some nights the Germans would drop various things. They dropped metal prongs that no matter how they fell on the ground, there would be one sharp prong straight up. In the tall grass, they could blow tires when taxiing a plane. They also dropped booby trap pens and pencils. You pick one up, unscrew it, and you lose a couple of hands. I was sitting at the

Fighter pilots look at a 487th Bomb Squadron, 340th Bomb Group B-25 in amazement just after the Mitchell crash landed on the 31st Fighter Group runway at Pomigliano, Italy. The left engine was ripped off and several of the crew were hurt. It was one thing to fly escort for the bombers and quite another to see up close what happened when they had been shot up. *William J. Skinner*

26

Jerry Carver stands in front of Bill Skinner's 308th Squadron Spit
Lonesome Polecat, Pomigliano, Italy, 1944. *William J. Skinner*

Donald Firoved and Ralph Francis use their Spitfire for some relaxation while waiting for engine start time before a mission. *William J. Skinner*

Though the Spitfire was smaller than most fighters, ground crew with a will could find a way to get into even the most difficult spaces, as these 308th Fighter Squadron men prove. *William J. Skinner*

When the 308th Fighter Squadron's ground crew managed to get a relatively undamaged Italian training plane airworthy, it became their own to do with as they wished. Pilots taught a few enlisted men how to fly it, and from then on, it was for enlisted men only—and they flew it

with great enthusiasm. Officers look on at Pomigliano, Italy, as *Achtung* is run up during a maintenance check. So successful was this effort that the aircraft went from field to field as the group moved, remaining an enlisted hack until it wore out. *William J. Skinner*

28

flagpole base and noticed a fountain pen on the ground. I told the guy with me to back off, took out my .45 automatic and hit it first shot. It was a perfectly good pen.

Barrie Davis, *P-51 pilot, 325th Fighter Group*

New pilots coming to our fighter group were invariably cocky to the point that they were dangerous to themselves. They thought the Luftwaffe was finished and that the P-51 could quickly and easily kill anything else that flew. To modify the attitude of newcomers, we used a war

Examining a newly arrived Merlin engine still mounted in the crate, 308th Fighter Squadron CO Maj. Walt Overend (right), Lieutenant Rodmyre (kneeling) and Lieutenant Roche waste no time in getting it assigned to one of the unit's Spitfires. *William J. Skinner*

weary P-40 which our squadron somehow acquired. I was in charge of putting new pilots through a quick, intensive training program, and the final flight included a mock dogfight with the new pilot of a P-51 pitted against one of us flying the P-40. I can tell you that until a pilot knows the strengths and weaknesses of both airplanes, the P-40 can make the P-51 look outclassed. Using all of the P-40's strengths, an innovative pilot could outfly a P-51 at low altitudes until the P-51 jockey finally realized that there was something more to fighting in the air than simply having the best airplane. At that point the new pilot became ready to listen to everything we had to say.

Paul Wingert, *P-38 pilot, 14th Fighter Group*

Flying at 10,000 feet, the squadron was greeted with a heavy barrage of flak. The squadron commander immediately started evasive action, but on the second barrage my aircraft was hit. I nursed it along as far as possible but within a few minutes both engines were dead. Not knowing my exact position, I rolled the aircraft over and bailed out, hoping I was over friendly territory. Falling for what seemed like eternity, I was able to locate the D-ring and gave it a hard pull. When the

The 308th Fighter Squadron chow line at Castel Volturno, Italy, February 1944. Everyone was still living in tents but at least the food got better when the Allies became established on the mainland. *William J. Skinner*

30

parachute opened, I was falling in a head-down position, causing it to stream and the shroud lines to wrap around my legs. With the chute streaming overhead I started to work frantically to untangle my legs—after getting them off I was then able to turn upright in the harness.

Tugging frantically on the shroud lines, I managed to make the parachute flare open, abruptly slowing my descent. By the time the chute opened properly, I was less than a thousand feet above the ground with very little time to orient myself—could only hope for the best as the ground came up to meet me.

An American infantry squad, for days in the mud of Italy with nothing but cold rations, were lining up for their first hot meal. As the cook yelled, "Come and get it," I landed at the head of the chow line. Dazed and shaken up from the bailout and somewhat hard landing, I still knew a good thing when I saw it so I unbuckled my chute harness, brushed myself off, smiled a big smile to everyone, picked up a mess kit and proceeded to be the first one through the chow line. I had parachuted into friendly territory by about half a mile.

Jack Lenox, *P–38 pilot, 14th Fighter Group*

I flew my third mission as wingman to group commander Col. O. B. Taylor. During a dive onto a formation of Me 109s I made a turn to

A 307th Fighter Squadron, 31st Fighter Group Spitfire Mk. IX sits ready for the day's mission. *William J. Skinner*

the left, losing sight of my leader. I observed black smoke trailing from the Me 109 I was firing at, but was unable to observe more as I continued my dive to outrun a 109 firing at me. Passing through about 15,000 feet, I was able to pull out of my dive and blacked out in the dive recovery. The next thing I knew, I was at 20,000 feet, alone, and trying to find someone to attach myself to. Seeing another P-38 in the same predicament, I

Lt. Bill Skinner, 308th Fighter Squadron, sits in his Spitfire awaiting the order to "press" and start engines in the early morning, Italy, 1944.
William J. Skinner

joined formation with the P-38 as his wingman and discovered it was the group commander! When we returned home, Col. Taylor commented on how we had become involved in the fight, and although he was all over the sky I had followed him and ended up in place on his wing. Of course I had no idea he was in the other P-38—all I was looking for was a wing to nest on.

Thomas H. Jones, *P-38 pilot, 82nd Fighter Group*

I well remember my first mission. After take-off and climb over the sea, some jock above and ahead of me cleared his four .50s with a burst of fire, as we always did, and the empty casings rattled off my windscreen, scaring the hell out of me. Thought the Jerries had me zeroed in and I was gonna be shot down!

12 February 1944. Bill Skinner's wingman stands in front of his leader's Spitfire Mk. VIII after landing at Castel Volturno, Italy, and points to the second kill he has just helped Skinner make. Victories were often hard to come by; this was the only kill made by an American pilot in the Mediterranean Theater that day. There was good reason for the wide smile. *William J. Skinner*

33

In March 1944 Mt. Vesuvius erupted and covered the surrounding area with lava cinders, destroying the 340th Bomb Group's B–25s near Pompeii and generally doing more damage than all the Luft- waffe's air raids. This was the view from Naples harbor. *William J. Skinner*

In March 1944, at Castel Volturno Airfield, Italy, the 308th Fighter Squadron lets go of its beloved Spitfires for new Mustangs, and are assigned a new mission. With the arrival of P-51s the 31st Group was transferred from the Twelfth to the Fifteenth Air Force for long range bomber escort duties which would take the group into combat over Germany itself. Though the P-51B and the unit's Spitfires both had Packard-built Rolls-Royce Merlin engines, the differences in the two aircraft are manifold. *William J. Skinner*

American Spitfire pilots with the 31st Fighter Group get a look at their first replacement P-51B at Castel Volturno, Italy, March 1944. The Mustang opened up the long range escort mission for the unit's pilots but they were not enthusiastic in the least about losing their maneuverable Spits. It would take some time and an increasing opportunity to shoot down enemy aircraft to make them forget the elegant British fighter. *William J. Skinner*

Bill Skinner's crew chief, Donald Firoved, and armorer, Ralph Francis, stand by their faithful *Lonesome Polecat* without much concern for the P–51B running up in the background. It was hard on all 31st Fighter Group personnel to let go of their proven Spitfires. *William J. Skinner*

Heading out from Foggia, Italy, for a mission with the 97th Squadron, 82nd Fighter Group are Lt. Billie B. Watson, Maj. Steve Stone and Capt. George Marvin. *Walter E. Zurney*

An 82nd Fighter Group Lightning departs from Foggia, Italy, on a
bomber escort mission in 1944. *Walter E. Zurney*

Flying from the mud and shacks of Foggia, Italy, *Taffy* was 1st Lt. Walter Zurney's 97th Squadron, 82nd Fighter Group Lightning—and his second love. *Walter E. Zurney*

Mud, mud, mud . . . Foggia, Italy, during the spring thaw of 1944. P-38 maintenance was never easy, but the weather often made it close to impossible. Work stands would sink into the gumbo and aircraft would be bogged down into a mush that could swallow things forever. Ground crews would wear a set of oversize boots out to the plane, then leave them on the ground or on the stands before stepping up onto the wing or into the cockpit. This P-38J of the 48th Squadron, 14th Fighter Group, has seen its share of use, and there hasn't been enough time to paint the right spinner. *Ira Latour*

1st Lt. Walter Zurney sits in his P-38 after his fiftieth and last mission. Zurney was one of the rare breed of sergeant pilots later commissioned as flight officers before going off to combat. *Walter E. Zurney*

A red-tailed P-51D of the all-black 301st Fighter Squadron, 332nd Fighter Group in November 1944. Though segregated from their fellow fighter pilots and often subjected to biased criticism, as 332nd pilot Louis R. Purnell recalled, "When you fly, nothing else matters. I could have been flying for the devil and it wouldn't have mattered." Not one bomber was lost in the time the 332nd provided escort for the Fifteenth Air Force's bomb groups. *Fred Bamberger via David W. Menard*

Fred F. Ohr's 2nd Fighter Squadron, 52nd Fighter Group P-51D with his six kills stenciled on the side. Originally equipped with reverse lend-lease Spitfires and sent from England to the Mediterranean, the 52nd later converted to Mustangs and became a part of the long-range escort units covering the Fifteenth Air Force. *Fred Bamberger via David W. Menard*

Chapter 3

Brother, It Was Rough in the ETO

Erwin Miller, *P-47 pilot, 4th Fighter Group*

When we strapped into a Spitfire we felt snug and part of the aircraft; the Thunderbolt cockpit, on the other hand, was so large that we felt if we slipped off the god damned seat we could break a leg! We were horrified at the thought of going to war in such a machine: we had enough trouble with the Focke-Wulfs in our nimble Spitfire Mk. Vs; now this lumbering seven-ton monster seemed infinitely worse.

Gradually, however, we learned how to fight in the Thunderbolt. At high altitude, she was a "hot ship" and very fast in a dive; if anyone tried to escape from a Thunderbolt by diving, we had him cold. Even more important, at last we had a fighter with the range to penetrate deeply into enemy territory—where the action was. So, reluctantly, we had to give up our beautiful little Spitfires and convert to the new juggernauts. The war was moving on and we had to move with it.

My heart remained with the Spitfire. The mere sound or sight of a Spitfire brings deep feelings. She was such a gentle little airplane, without a trace of viciousness. She was a dream to handle in the air.

Arthur L. Thorsen, *P-38 pilot, Eighth AF Replacement Training Unit*

I had always felt that getting shot down was part of this game and I dwelt on that possibility so much it began to disturb my sleep. I was having a recurring nightmare that started one night on the *Aquatania*, during the crossing. The dream would begin peacefully enough with me at the controls of a P-38 and in a group formation with other ships, penetrating enemy territory. Suddenly we were under attack by Jerries and we careened around the sky, firing, turning, and spinning out.

I was on the tail of a Focke-Wulf 190 and was just getting my sights lined up when the loud banging of machine gun bullets on metal started tearing my aircraft apart. I had not kept my tail clear and another Jerry was making me pay for the blunder. As my ship began disintegrating, I popped the canopy and nonchalantly stepped out into space. I fell for a few seconds and then seeing that I was clear of the debris I pulled the ripcord of my parachute. A few seconds passed, nothing happened, no parachute. Now frantic, I twisted my head and looked up to see what was wrong with the chute. A cold hand clutched at my gizzard, for there was no parachute—just dirty laundry streaming from my back pack. Long johns, dirty socks, pillow cases, even a red nightshirt.

As always, I awoke with a snort, clammy sweat covering my body. I felt I was getting a heavenly message and swore I would never bail out. I made a pact with myself that, should the time come when I was shot up badly, I would not leave the aircraft as long as there was a response of any kind from the controls. After all, P-38s belly in just as easy as they land on wheels.

42

Sunset at Nuthampstead, the 55th Fighter Group's initial home with the Eighth Air Force in England. *Robert T. Sand*

Socked in at Wormingford, 22 December 1944. This 55th Fighter Group P-51D's crew chief was Roger Fraleigh, assisted by Nick Lippucci. Fraleigh was awarded a medal for his aircraft flying the most missions without mechanical failure. The Mustang was later lost in action on 20 February 1945. *Robert T. Sand*

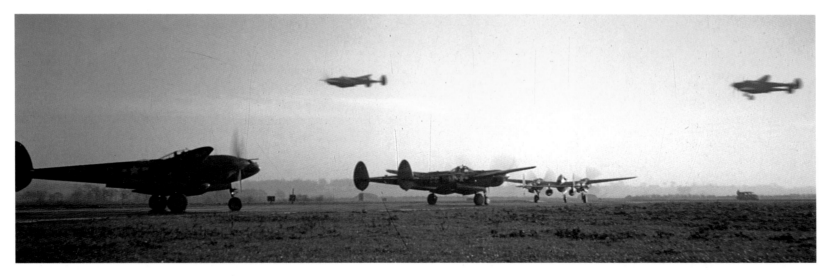

55th Fighter Group Lightnings taxi out and take off on a mission in late December 1943. Pilots were already numb with frosted instruments and fingers, then had to climb into the minus 50 degree Fahrenheit temperature at altitude with virtually no cockpit heat. "This was always an agonizing moment for all," said Bob Sand, "particularly at this period, as the Allison engines and Curtiss electric propellers were not as dependable as the [P-51's] Merlins and Hamilton props. This agony was particularly true for the propeller men. The chief and crew could turn away when they saw their ship take off, then pray that all would go well for the hours ahead, and to a safe return. Only then was he sure he had done everything right to protect the life of his pilot. The propeller men, however, could not rest easy until *every ship* was off safely and had returned safely. And when *any* ship was lost unaccountably, there remained a little nagging question." *Robert T. Sand*

Herbert E. Johnson, *P–38 pilot, 20th Fighter Group*

The P–38 requires a far greater knowledge of its mechanical and aerodynamic characteristics on the part of the pilot than normally required to fly fighters.

If jumped on the deck the best evasive maneuver is a tight level turn. Due to the beautiful stall characteristics of the '38, you can turn much tighter without the danger of spinning than any German craft.

Hubert "Hub" Zemke, *P–38, P–47 and P–51 pilot and fighter group commander*

I was fortunate enough to have flown the P–51, P–47 and P–38 in combat and to have led fighter groups with all three.

P–51—By far the best air-to-air fighter aircraft of the three below 25,000 feet. A very good long-range radius of action for the type of work

we did in Europe. The acceleration from slow cruise to maximum performance was excellent compared to the competition.

Its rate of roll was good and it maneuvered easily to a learned hand. Dive and acceleration were rapid. Visibility in all directions was very ample for the need. As an instrument aircraft it was a bit touchy. It could be overactive in turbulence.

On armament it carried sufficient machine guns. Why I say this is that after viewing numerous combat films where pilots often fired at extreme range or overdeflected, I came firmly to the conclusion that one fought for a combat position of 10 degrees or less deflection. At close range—250 yards or less—there is no doubt what could happen when the trigger was depressed. It was a matter of ducking the flying pieces after that. This was drilled into the skulls of all pilots.

P–47—A rugged beast with a sound radial engine to pull you along.

Heavy in fire power that chewed up the opponent at close ranges. Best suited and likewise adopted in the ground support role, as everything in the armament arsenal was hung on its sturdy wings.

Accelerated poorly and climbed not too much better from a slow airspeed. Once a good high cruising speed was attained, the P–47 could pretty well stand up with the competition.

Strangely the rate of roll and maneuverability was good at high speeds. In fact, the aircraft had many a forgiving feature and reliability. With its high altitude supercharger its performance at altitude—above 24,000 to 25,000—appeared superior to the other two U.S. Army Air Corps fighters in the theater. At high altitude this fighter's level speed, better climb and more solid response to control reflected the tactics that the 56th Fighter Group developed early in combat.

Swinging the compass on a 55th Fighter Group P–38 at Nuthampstead, dawn, 2 January 1944. *Robert T. Sand*

It should not be overlooked here that the P-47—once it gained altitude—could exceed any of the contenders in speed of entering a dive with a very good "zoom" recovery to altitude again.

Naturally, a fighter pilot endeavors to fight his aircraft from the strengths of his machine's performance rather than from its weaknesses. With this in mind, I repeatedly impressed upon the 56th's fighter pilots that our tactics were to "hit and recover, hit and recover." If one couldn't get the opponent by an altitude of 15,000 feet, then break off and recover to altitude again.

In this respect it was stressed that the element leader, who initiated the attack, pressed in viciously. If he missed his attack, it was his responsibility to set up his wingman to press through for a cleanup kill on the dive. If the wingman's follow-through failed, a zoom recovery by the element leader to give high cover and a position for a second attack often resulted.

This one, two punch tactic was continued into refinement of the entire

20th Fighter Group Lightnings at Wittering in December 1943 when the type was new to the ETO. Harry Bisher's *Kitty* is the second aircraft from the left. *Air Force Museum*

The 364th Fighter Group lines up for takeoff at Honington, England, in the late summer of 1944. The tension generated by pre-mission jitters would normally give way to a sense of power as the Merlin engines were run up to 61 in. of manifold pressure and 3000 rpm for takeoff. From that point on, leaders were intent on joining with the other flights, and wingmen had no other world but keeping tight formation from brake release until ready to scan for bogies once in enemy territory. *Mark H. Brown/USAFA*

group's tactical employment, wherein the first or lead squadron was designated the Assault or Strike squadron, the second designated Support or Follow Through squadron which flew a bit higher, and the third which flew still higher, became the Reserve or High Cover Squadron.

Though the 56th received criticism for this conservative policy of not bouncing below 15,000 feet, until the introduction of the paddle blade propeller and water injection to the R-2800 engine there was considerable effort to refine tactics and coordination of the entire group formation. The tactic worked.

About the highest engagement I recall was just over 35,000 feet. Here the P-47 still performed fairly well while the enemy (Me 109s) had dropped off considerably. In about one turn with the group, the opponents were falling off in spins or split-S-ing for denser air mass. Then the enemy fell into the trap of being overhauled by the superior diving speed of the P-47. The P-51 and P-38 also employed these tactics but to a lesser degree in dive performance to the P-47.

As an instrument flying platform, the P-47 proved to be better than the

A brand-new P-51D upon arrival at the 355th Fighter Group's home base of Steeple Morden, England, mid-1944. The only markings applied at the air depots after assembly were black bands on wings and tail and a black nose. *Alexander C. Sloan via Bob Kuhnert, 355th FG Assn.*

P-51 but probably not as good as the P-38. Though not equipped for icing conditions, with carburetor heat the engine pulled the bulk through.

As to fire power, the eight .50 caliber machine guns were ample proof of a real punch either in aerial combat or on a strafing run. Once dive bombing was learned, the P-47 consistently came up with flying colors.

P-38—Though this aircraft had virtues, for me it was the poorest of the three U.S. Army fighters in the European Theater. The fact that the extreme cold at altitude affected its performance hardly endears the machine. The turbosuperchargers were controlled by an oil regulator. At altitude the oil had a tendency to congeal, which caused serious

Though all bubble canopy Mustangs were delivered natural metal without camouflage paint, there was skepticism about flying shiny aluminum aircraft that flashed in the sun like mirrors. The 357th Group decided to paint its aircraft in the field, sometimes in regulation olive drab and other times in RAF green which was made available by the English. Clearly, Julian H. Bertram's *Butch Boy* got this treatment when Joe Broadhead flew it as *Master Mike*. Note the chipped paint and the long stream of oil from the engine breather exit below the word "Butch." *Alexander C. Sloan via Bob Kuhnert, 355th FG Assn.*

Lt. Marvin W. Arthur with his *Blondie* at Debden, England, home of the 4th Fighter Group. As crew chief Don Allen remembered, "We were supposed to use kerosene to wash oil and soot off the planes, but it usually wasn't on site . . . thus we took a bucket of 140 octane gas and washed the junk off. It's a wonder we weren't all blown sky high. Youth . . . thinks it's invulnerable!" *Donald E. Allen*

Thunderbolts from the 78th Fighter Group just after landing; external tanks are gone, a Mae West is hanging on the machine guns, pilots are donning A-2 jackets (which were worthless for flying in the frigid higher altitudes) and walking off the kinks from sitting cramped up for so long. The paddle-bladed propellers shown here resulted in a major performance increase for the P-47, giving much improved rate of climb and acceleration. *Mark H. Brown/USAFA*

Maj. Claiborne H. Kinnard, Jr.'s first *Man O' War* just after the 354th Fighter Squadron commander got his first kill on 29 March 1944. The standard ETO white nose and bands on wing and tail have been applied, as well as the Malcolm Hood over the cockpit in place of the factory-installed "chicken coop" panels. The white paint was supposed to help identify American fighters from their German counter-

parts, but aircraft continued to be lost to friendly fire. The Spitfire-style bubble canopy was a major improvement that pilots found outstanding in all respects, allowing them to actually lean out over the canopy rail and look behind. *Alexander C. Sloan via Bob Kuhnert, 355th FG Assn.*

problems. On two occasions I recall, when entering combat with enemy single seaters it was a case of life and death to get away and survive, though I had started with the advantage.

On both occasions the engines either cut out completely or overran rpm limitations as the throttles were cut or advanced. It was enough just to regulate the engines and control the aircraft without entering combat.

The second serious limiting factor that detracted from the P-38's combat capability was its steep diving restriction—estimated at about 375 mph. A common tactic of the Luftwaffe single seaters was to split-S for the clouds or the deck. Oftentimes their head-on attacks on the bomber formations saw them roll over and dive for the deck to confuse and outdistance the flexible machine gunners. P-38s had little chance to pursue. When on defense, it can be easily understood that a dive to safety was the best maneuver for longevity.

Another factor to degrade the P-38's combat capability was its identification factor. The eyes of a pilot often picked up specks in the distance that could not be immediately identified as friend or foe. These were reported in as "bogies." Appropriate tactical maneuvers were taken to prevent bogies from having the advantage of a subsequent attack. In the case of the P-38 the twin booms and slab elevator gave this aircraft's identity away—as far as the eye could see.

It was also necessary for the P-38 pilot to do much more weaving to look down over the two engines that lay on each side of the cockpit. A better cockpit heating system could

have been provided as my feet always froze at altitude.

Taken alone, the above statements would conclude that the P-38 had no outstanding features . . . it did! As a gun platform, it was steady as a shooting stand. With two engines, there was no torque. With a little trim for buildup of speed (in a dive), a pilot could ride directly into a target.

As to the armament installation, I have seen no better. Four machine guns and one cannon in a tight pocket directly in front of the pilot. This armament being so closely aligned to the sight of plane of the gunsight required no convergence of fire as necessitated in fighters having their guns placed in the wings.

Though the P-38 had a wheel instead of the proverbial stick, this was no handicap—controls were light and response was excellent.

Relative to load carrying capacity, the aircraft could take off with just about anything. I've taken off with a thousand pound bomb under each wing and cruised with ease. On fuel consumption, the P-38 enabled us to cruise out to combat areas deep in Germany without the anguish of not having enough "petrol" to return home.

A tricycle landing gear made it much easier for a junior pilot to "spike the kite" on the runway and chalk up another landing. This was also an advantage in taxiing—a large engine and cowling did not deter from forward vision.

Harrison B. Tordoff, *P-47 pilot, 353rd Fighter Group*

We loved the P-47 for its toughness and reliability. It was heavy and looked cumbersome but in the

hands of a good pilot, it could turn and climb with an Me 109 or an Fw 190. And nothing could outdive it. We had pilots bring back tree branches and tops of telephone poles in the wings of their '47s. A few even came home with top cylinders shot off. It could be belly landed in a forest, if necessary. On an open field, it crash-landed about as well as it landed on wheels. Pilots learn to appreciate this sort of toughness. The eight .50 caliber machine guns were devastating on ground or air targets and the plane was a very stable gun platform. On the negative side, the '47 burned fuel at full power at 450 gallons/hour, if I remember right. It only carried about 350 gallons internally. It got nose light in a stall, and nose heavy in a dive—had a very nasty spin—violent and hard to stop. I spun out of a slow turn at high altitude with full wing tanks once, by accident, while trying to keep in formation on a combat mission. It tore the wing tanks off and scared hell out of me. But the general way I felt in a '47 was invincible. I had complete faith in the plane and would excuse its shortcomings to anyone.

Marvin Bledsoe, *P-47 pilot, 353rd Fighter Group (from his book* Thunderbolt, *Van Nostrand Reinhold, 1982)*

The target for the day was a railroad tunnel that the heavy bombers had been unable to destroy. The Germans were rushing reinforcements toward the beachhead at night, using this particular railroad track. The fighters' job was to go in low and destroy the tunnel.

The air was charged with excitement when we entered the

briefing room. I was nervous, my insides kept whirling around, and I was scared as hell. The instant the briefing was over I raced for the latrine, where I felt my stomach turning inside out.

As we headed to our planes my mouth was dry. I found it hard to breathe and almost impossible to swallow. My stomach was doing flip-flops; I was terrified.

In the cockpit of the Thunderbolt I felt somewhat better. How I loved to fly that airplane!

This takeoff of our fighter squadron was a thrilling spectacle. Every engine started at the same moment in one huge roar. The planes taxied out toward the runway in close formation, then seemed to pause and huddle together at the extreme end, wing tips and twirling props bare inches from the ships next to them. Each squadron lined up on a different runway, waiting its turn to take off. When the last airplane of the first squadron started down, the group

Cameron Hart's 63rd Fighter Squadron P-47D warms up in the foreground as the 56th Fighter Group lines up for takeoff from Boxted, England, in late 1944. It was not unusual for variations of the squadron insignia to be used for nose art, as can be seen on Hart's Thunderbolt. *Mark H. Brown/USAFA*

52

operations officer fired a flare from the tower, signaling the second squadron to give their engines the gun. They crossed the intersection an instant behind the last ship that had taken off on the other runway.

My flight leader's ship taxied by and I moved into position alongside

him. My ground crew gave me a final "thumbs up" as we headed out to the runway.

The frightened feeling had passed. I felt a surge of pride that I was a member of a combat fighter squadron and was flying the most powerful fighter ship in the world.

Chet A Patterson, *P–38 pilot, 55th Fighter Group*

Because of the losses in P–38 units someone at Lockheed thought the pilots didn't known how to fly it so they sent over Tony LeVier. As far as I was concerned, he did nothing that I couldn't do or nothing that I hadn't

56th Fighter Group commander Col. David C. Schilling's P-47D fitted with rocket tubes for the increasing ground attack work that took place after D-Day. When the 56th elected to remain the only Eighth Air Force fighter group flying Thunderbolts after the rest transitioned to Mustangs, a number of non-standard and colorful camouflage schemes began to appear in place of the GI-issue olive drab and gray or natural metal. Not only did it set the Wolfpack apart, but it served as a vent for artistic license in trying out the effective use of paint in combat. *Mark H. Brown/USAFA*

Sheep in wolf's clothing—a P-47 of the 65th Fighter Wing Detachment B, Air-Sea Rescue Squadron, at Boxted in Mid-1944. Later redesignated the 5th Emergency Rescue Squadron, the unit was equipped with war-weary (note WW on tail) P-47Ds to drop smoke markers and dinghy packs near downed airmen. Though not quite as glamorous as flying fighters in combat, the unit did an exceptional job, flying an effective 3,520 of 3,616 sorties in aiding some very desperate men. *Mark H. Brown/USAFA*

The 335th Fighter Squadron dispersal area, 4th Fighter Group home base, Debden, with the sun low on the horizon. With drop tanks hung, canopies open and engines run up, last-minute polishing of windscreens takes place as the "kites" are being readied for the next "show." *Joseph B. Sills*

seen around the airfield by our own men. Had it been my choice of what he did, I would have had him fly some two hours at 28,000 feet, then tangle with me at 15,000 feet instantly. Then

we would see how well he could fly when he was frozen.

As an example, Bushing, who did not like combat, was up leading the 338th Squadron and had to urinate.

Well, by the time you got out of your shoulder harness, the parachute straps and through four more layers of clothes (tank suit, pinks, long johns and shorts) you found your peter was

Up for some proficiency time on 2 June 1945, almost a month after the war in Europe ended, 354th Fighter Squadron, 355th Fighter Group pilots fight to hold formation in some very rough air. From front to back: Stan Silva in WR-B *My Catherine*, WR-V, WR-S (bar), Clay Kinnard's former WR-A, WR-T (bar), Glenn Beeler in WR-L (bar),

Don Langley in WR-C *Lil Curly Top*. Just outside camera range were Jimmy Jabara in WR-P (bar) and James O'Neill. Moments later they had a mid-air and both managed to bail out successfully. *Alexander C. Sloan via Bob Kuhnert, 355th FG Assn.*

about one half inch long at that altitude. Well anyway, Bushing let go in the relief tube and at that very moment someone hollered, "Bogies on the right!" Bushing turned to the right and madly looked for the bogies, and though it was a false alarm, by the time his heart stopped pumping and he looked back at the dashboard, he could see only frosted instruments.

To be sure things were working properly, he had to take off his gloves and with his fingernails scrape off the frost on the important instruments. When he got back to the field the P-38, once it got on the ground, turned into a hot box even in England. So by the time he taxied up to the hard stand and shut down the engines the urine had melted and heated up to probably 110 degrees. By tradition, the crew chief climbed on the aircraft as soon as you killed the engines and opened the canopy. In this case, just as

With a puff of oil smoke, Lieutenant Erickson cranks up the 55th Fighter Group Lightning normally assigned to Capt. Jerry H. Ayers.
Robert T. Sand

Capt. Jerry Ayers' P-38 gets a going over at Nuthampstead in late
1943. *Robert T. Sand*

he opened it, he slammed it down when he got a whiff of what was there. Bushing had not noticed it as he had been wearing his oxygen mask.

Edward B. Giller, *P–38 pilot, 55th Fighter Group*

Returning to England with considerable undercast always presented a severe problem of location. We had only four channels of VHF which were always crowded. Once over England we could only let down straight ahead until you could see the ground. The other P–38 groups were operating with the same problem as the 55th. But one thing we liked about the P–38 was its instrument flying ability.

Flying around 30,000 feet resulted in extreme fouling of the plugs in the Allison engine as well as a great number of thrown rods and swallowed valves. Needless to say, a P–38 on a single engine was in an unenviable condition. Our record during this period was very poor, about 1.5 Germans shot down to each American lost to all causes.

This was the world's coldest airplane and we tried every combination of suit, glove and heater imaginable, including some that

Phil Savides, suited up and ready to go at the 313th Squadron, 50th Fighter Group parachute shop in Nancy, France, 1944. The Ninth Air Force's Thunderbolts flew some of the most effective, and most dangerous, ground support missions of the war. *Phil Savides*

Lt. George D. Green, 4th Fighter Group, with his Mustang in mid-1944. When squadron mate Pierce McKennon bailed out of his P-51 near Berlin on 18 March 1945, Green set his P-51 down in a nearby field, threw the chute out, put McKennon in the seat, got on his lap and took off. Sharing one oxygen mask, they made it all the way back to Debden. *USAF/NASM*

would short out and give you a hot foot. We were so cold sometimes, we did not even want to fight.

The twin tails provided positive recognition for the Germans at distances greater than we could see them. Therefore, our initial engagements were always at a disadvantage. We were forced to go to very high altitudes, 30,000 feet to 35,000 feet. Even so, the Germans flew way above us. The Germans would escape by a split-S maneuver from these altitudes and the P-38 could not follow due to compressibility.

The maintenance on the P-38 was something to behold. The engines were extremely closely-cowled with much piping and no space. The mechanics did a magnificent job with extremely long hours of trying tediously to fix coolant leaks, rough engines, etc. It was truly a crew chief's nightmare. The plane employed oleo shocks on all three landing gear struts. These had a habit of leaking as soon as it got cold and required considerable maintenance to reinflate. The turbo supercharger regulator had a delightful habit of freezing at high altitude, resulting in only two throttle settings . . . 10 inches of mercury, which would not sustain flight, or 80 inches which would blow up a supercharger. I recall one very cold day over the Ruhr Valley [in Germany] where both the pilots and the regulators were so frozen that, in spite of heavy flak in that vicinity, we let down to 3,000 feet to warm up both us and the airplanes.

Harry R. Corey, *P-51 pilot, 339th Fighter Group*

Weather, the other enemy, is a factor in any form of combat. The Romans built roads in Britain, not out of civic pride, but to increase the mobility of their legions. Air combat involves a third dimension, because the cloud cover can range from 100 to over 2,000 feet. Winds aloft, that can reach 70 to 90 mph, are a fourth dimension. We lost eleven pilots (thirteen planes) due to adverse weather. This was more than we lost to the Luftwaffe. Seven pilots had less than two months of combat experience. Five of these were operational for one month or less. Frequently missions were flown without ever seeing the ground between take off and landing. If coupled with the loss of radio contact, this could lead to disaster.

We lost two pilots under these same circumstances. It was a long mission (7 hours) to Posnan, Poland. (One element became separated from its squadron during combat and were last heard from in the direction of

Maj. Pierce W. "Mac" McKennon's P-51D on the line at Debden with the 335th Squadron, 4th Fighter Group. This was the second of his *Ridge Runner* Mustangs with the Arkansas razorback on the side and his string of victories. On 18 March 1945 he bailed out of this fighter near Berlin and was picked up by Gearge Green. *Joseph B. Sills*

Though similar in appearance to his earlier Mustangs, Pierce McKennon's *Ridge Runner III* had a slightly different razorback hog, more victory markings and the two parachutes added for his successful escapes after going down in enemy territory. Here Mac poses with his colorful mount just after it replaced the one he left in Germany. This aircraft was eventually crash-landed in France on 17 April 1945 by another pilot. *Joseph B. Sills*

Southampton.) They called for a bearing to our base, which was forty degrees or northeast. Their transmission was weak and they did not respond. Their leader's receiver may have been out, or more likely, they were too low over the Channel to receive. The English Channel is only 110 miles south of our base. A strong wind from the north could easily cause them to drift that far south during a long mission. They went out to sea with very little fuel left.

After an escort mission to Halle, near Leipzig, the bombers returned via

Front office—the wartime cockpit of a P–38J Lightning. On the left are the red-balled throttles, prop pitch controls and mixture levers. Behind the control yoke in the center is the main switch box and armament selectors with the magneto switches on the upper left. The machine gun and cannon triggers are on the wheel grips, while the red dive flap switch is on the left brace and the white microphone button is on the right brace. The printed placards on the yoke are dive limiting speeds (left) and power and flap settings (right). The flap handle is just to the right of the yoke, mounted on the right side of the cockpit just in front of the radio and electrical controls. Oxygen regulator and controls are mounted on the center floor between the rudder pedals.

a southern route. Our escort left them at Hersfeld, south of Kassel. They made landfall out near Dieppe, on the deck under a 100% cloud cover. This put them on a northerly course for home across the English Channel. All three pilots in one flight were lost when they apparently came upon the cliffs of the Isle of Wight too late to successfully pull up. They must have spun in, as one was found on the Isle, one on the beach at low tide, and the third crashed near Nuthampstead.

The Cliffs of Dover presented a similar hazard. However, most pilots still favored coming home on the deck when the weather was bad. If we let down over East Anglia we would be competing for space with a few hundred bombers and other fighters. If you happened to go past the base before breaking out you could meet up with a barrage balloon. The most important key was to establish a rate of descent (or climb) before entering the clouds. This relieved pressure on the controls and helped to avoid the very slow imperceptible movements that can confuse your inner ear, cause vertigo and put the seat of your pants in conflict with your instruments. Half of our losses can be attributed to vertigo. During the let down we would call home for a heading from our homing station and get an altimeter setting. In addition to correcting for any change in pressure, it provided a slight margin for error because our base was about 50 feet above sea level.

It was also a good idea to have an alternate plan in case the radio failed. My system was to pick up the main road from Norwich to London. Turn left down the road until I came to my special roundabout. Then a hard

right due west for two minutes, let down the gear, flaps and look for a green flare. On one occasion, I had to warn my flight that there was a Jug [P-47] in our traffic pattern. Then, once again, we were safely down on that good old grass field. Except that this time we were at Duxford! Their folks were kind enough to point out the direction to Fowlmere, about four miles west.

Of course one could fly 5 minutes in any direction in East Anglia and find an Air Base. This was very helpful on one mission when the ceiling was especially low. Capt. Richard Olander led Red Flight and I had White Flight tucked in behind and below so tightly that I was inside Red four. We came down from 20,000 feet and shortly after we made land fall, we came over the end of a paved runway. They were shooting up green flares. Olander called for us to take spacing for landing and no one argued. We made one circle keeping the field off my left wing tip. When I got back to the flares we set them down. I was enjoying the roll and the cool breeze, when I saw them on my left. The other four planes had landed on the second runway and we were heading for the intersection. Fortunately, we had good spacing so that a little throttle allowed us to alternate every other plane at the intersection. It was show time at Wormingford, near Colchester, which we subsequently learned was the home of the 55th FG. After we came inside and the coffee was poured, their control tower officer came in with the startling news that we had landed on intersecting runways! Someone in the back of the room said, "We always land that way at a strange field." That

plus the hot coffee had reduced the adrenaline levels and chased from our minds any thoughts of what might have been or how narrow the margin between success and disaster can be.

Robert T. Sand, *Propeller shop, 55th Fighter Group*
Sometimes, for reasons I don't know—probably an unseated gas cap—the P-38 would start syphoning out its gasoline. From the ground it looked like a long plume of mist coming from the wing.

One day, as the planes were droning around the field getting into formation for a mission, a group of ground crew members were in the radio shack listening to the conversations of the pilots. Suddenly, they heard this: "Pete, you'll have to abort! You are syphoning fuel!" No answer. Then, a little more urgently, "Pete! Abort! Abort! You are syphoning fuel!" Finally a sheepish voice came on, "Aw hell. No I'm not. I forgot to go to the bathroom and I'm just taking a leak."

Arthur L. Thorsen, *P-38 pilot, 55th Fighter Group*
We flew through a fierce anti-aircraft barrage and the gunners had just enough lead on [John] Landers to get me instead. Suddenly, amidst the deafening explosions, my aircraft was pitched nearly upside down. I don't know how I righted the ship so close to the ground without crashing. There must be some kind of unknown skill that surfaces in times of disaster to give your mind and body an instantaneous reaction impulse. I had no time to check my damage, for shells were exploding all around me. I pushed the nose forward, aware that I was using all my strength on the left

rudder, to keep the aircraft level. I was cutting the grass and went through what I perceived to be a baby fruit orchard, cutting saplings with the leading edge of my wing like they were stalks of sunflowers.

Eventually the firing ceased and I saw, with horror, that my right propeller had only one blade and was windmilling. I immediately cut the switch to that engine and trimmed the ship. Then I noticed blood dripping on my lap. I put my hand to my head and my right eyebrow felt mushy. My goggle was smashed. My left eye was stinging and I opened and closed each eye alternately. I could see! I looked at the right engine. It appeared to be gutted.

I couldn't believe it! I was helpless, with one engine shot out and no escort. Meat on the table for any Hun aircraft that should spot me . . . There was nothing else to do, but try to make it back to England alone, on one engine. If I get jumped on the way, I'll just bail out, hide in a haystack somewhere with an armload of cabbages and wait for the invasion. I put my hand on my forehead again.

The bleeding seemed to have stopped, but I had the impression my right eyebrow was gone.

With the ship trimmed up now, it seemed to be handling okay. I twisted my head to examine my plexiglas canopy. There were no holes in it. No holes anywhere in the cockpit that I could see, but some bits of flak must have come in from somewhere. I was on a compass heading of 290 degrees and doing 180 miles an hour. If I stayed on the deck, I might not be spotted. I saw the Meuse River coming up and the city of Namur on

Sitting in its hardstand at Boxted, *Pat* from the 56th Fighter Group's 63rd Fighter Squadron warms up for a mission in 1944. The black and white invasion stripes were painted on all Allied aircraft the night before D-Day in order to prevent friendly gunners from shooting at the wrong guys in the heat of battle. It still didn't seem to stop them. As the months went by and the Allies were firmly established on the Continent, the stripes slowly disappeared, first from the tops of the aircraft, then from the undersides of the wings and finally from below the fuselage. *Mark H. Brown/USAFA*

62

my right. I wasn't picking up flak anymore and surmised I was too low for the Jerry radar to detect me.

Time passed, my single engine droning smoothly. I was beginning to feel good. I passed between Brussels and Lille and was soon crossing out over the Channel at Dunkirk. I had made it! I was now approaching London and several Spitfires joined me, flying formation. The pilots studied my aircraft and then, with a wave, they were gone again. I hit the mike button and called Fusspot, our control at Wormingford. I explained my condition. They acknowledged and assigned me a specific runway to land on. Four miles from home! I had made it, but not quite!

Things started going wrong at that moment. I felt a lurch as my landing gear came down. I hadn't touched my landing gear lever. The extra drag was killing my air speed. I goosed the good engine and the aircraft wanted to roll. I couldn't use more power. I was going down! My altimeter read 800 feet! My nose was down too low and the ship wasn't responding to its elevators. I quickly locked my shoulder straps and rolled trim tabs, but too late. The ship was wobbling as the nose came up slightly, then I hit a telephone pole, snapping it like a match stick. It caromed me into another. It, too, snapped! I had the nose up, but the ship went skidding into the roof of some kind of building and I was lost in a shower of debris. Then the ship hit the ground and bounced up again, becoming engulfed in flying stones, dirt and several tons of turnips. I thought the ship would explode and released my harness and canopy, but as the ship bounced the canopy slammed back and drove me down into the cockpit again. My bell was rung, but I still knew what was going on and pushed the canopy up and scrambled free of the wreckage, still expecting it to explode. It didn't.

I managed to run about fifty feet from the crash and fell down. My legs didn't seem to want to work anymore. Suddenly I was aware of a civilian running to me. I started to yell a warning to him to stay back, the ship might explode, but then, I noticed he was carrying a bottle, which I took to be scotch, and decided to let him approach and we'd brave the explosion together. Right behind him came a lady I assumed to be his wife. She was carrying a cup of tea, and they commenced to arguing over what I should have, the scotch or the tea. I felt it incumbent upon me to settle this family argument, so I grabbed the bottle, took a long pull of what was, indeed, scotch and then washed it down with the tea. I smiled my thanks to both of them. . . . I had one last look

Lt. Robert Schmidt has just pulled the mixture on his *Tar Baby* after a mission with the 356th Fighter Group in April 1945. His crew chief is already up on the wing to get the first report of how the show went, and more importantly, to ask whether pilot had any "squawks" on the aircraft. *Herbert R. Rutland, Jr.*

A meeting of fighter group commanders at Debden on 23 March 1945 to plan support for the Rhine River crossing. In this lineup are Mustangs from the following groups: 359th, 20th, 353rd, 357th and an F-5 Lightning from the 7th Photo Group. *Edward B. Richie*

The next row of aircraft at Debden on 23 March 1945 were from these groups: 355th, 361st, 339th, 364th, 55th and 356th. Certainly VIII Fighter Command allowed their pilots to carry some of the most colorful markings since von Richthofen's Flying Circus. *Edward B. Richie*

at my dead bird, lying out there in the turnip patch. It had gotten me home with its last gasp. It was like saying goodbye to a very dear friend.

Elmer W. O'Dell, *P-51 pilot, 363rd Fighter Group*

I destroyed an aircraft on my first mission. Unfortunately, it was a P-51. I was taking off on my leader's wing when I blew a tire and swerved toward him. Kicking opposite rudder, I avoided the collision, but by the time I got straightened out I didn't have enough speed or runway to get airborne. I cut the switches, held the stick in my gut, and closed my eyes. The plane ran off the field, across the sunken road which sheared off the gear, dropped on two full wing tanks, skidded across a field, tore off the left wing on a stump, and wound up with its nose in a chicken coop. I was told later that I killed a crow in a hedge along the road and two chickens in the coop. The Mustang was rugged. I didn't even get a scratch.

Arthur L. Thorsen, *P-38 pilot, 55th Fighter Group*

As I shaved and showered for the Officer's Club dance, I thought how fortunate I was, being in the Army Air Corps. We fight a clean war. We have a change of clothes whenever we wish. We eat well. We sleep between

The 56th Fighter Group lines up for takeoff from Boxted. In the foreground Russell Westfall runs up his P-47D *Amaposa II. Mark H. Brown/USAFA*

sheets on soft mattresses, and we carry on at the Officer's Club after duty hours. We fly from four to six hours per mission and we're through for the day. We fly magnificent aircraft that we could never even climb into in civilian life and rarely do we see the bloody side of combat. The bomber crews do, but fighter pilots are alone and are spared that shock. If one of our pilots is wounded, he would faint from loss of blood, long before he could be attended to and crash in enemy territory. Without a doubt, this must have been what happened to many of our missing friends. But we had a habit of not accepting the loss of a comrade as final. We just said that he was transferred to another group. Apart from that, however, we led a good life.

Arthur L. Thorsen, *P-38 pilot, 55th Fighter Group*

With more experience I was becoming more comfortable with the job. My green was wearing off. It occurred to me that I was no longer trembling when I got into an airplane for a mission, but only when I was crawling out of the cockpit, after a mission. The mission briefings were no longer leaving an anvil in my stomach. Things were becoming routine, for I believe I convinced myself that the only Jerry that could clobber me would be the one I didn't see.

I hoped this attitude would continue. I was more afraid of doing something less than honorable, than I was of facing the German. I told myself I would never abort a mission, no matter how life threatening it was, unless I legitimately had mechanical problems. There were those, not only in my group, but other groups too, who would purposely ride their brakes, taxiing to the runway for a mission takeoff and have their brakes lock up, prohibiting a takeoff. Others would accidentally drop belly tanks on the taxi strip or imagine a more than 100 rpm mag drop upon running up their engines. Both cases sufficient reason to abort.

No one was really fooled, but even if these ploys worked, the pilot guilty of them had to live with his own conscience. I realized I was drawing closer to the men who flew the missions without complaint, or trickery. It was not a case of heroics on anyone's part, it was simply an attitude of, "If the other guys are doing it, so can I."

Arthur L. Thorsen, *P-38 pilot, 55th Fighter Group*

I ventured another look away from Wyche's ship. P-38s were assembling from all directions as we headed over the North Sea back to England. I was amazed at the outcome of [my first] mission. We tangled with the Germans, had a dogfight and I was still alive. How about that? It was strange how abruptly the fight ended. Then again, perhaps it wasn't. The Jerries could break combat anytime they wanted to by heading for the deck—which is what they did. Our job was to stay with the bombers until relieved. . . .

I was suddenly very hungry, and remembering a chocolate bar I had tucked away in the shin pocket of my flying suit, I reached down for it, unaware that, in so doing, I had pulled the yoke back into my lap. My ship climbed. When I straightened up and relaxed my hold on the yoke, the ship levelled off 500 feet above the group.

I looked around, a cold hand clutching my heart. There wasn't a ship in the sky! *My God!,* I thought. *Where is the group?* Perhaps something happened back at Kiel and the group turned back to give assistance. I was panic-stricken—all alone over the North Sea.

I made a steep 180 degree turn and headed back to the target area, then I heard a voice on the R/T. It was the Colonel.

"Who is that silly bastard that made a 180?" he inquired.

I knew that had to be me and I was elated at the sound of so friendly a voice. I made another 180 and could see the group 500 feet below and ahead of me. Saved! I pushed the throttles forward, dipped the nose and took my place next to Wyche as fast as I could.

Wyche came over the R/T very quietly, "Arthur, Arthur, Arthur," he chuckled.

Geez, I thought, how could I be so dumb? If I am to have any hope of surviving this war, I had better grow up fast. I had to be about the greenest of all the replacements that came with me to the 55th. How could any combat pilot be in a dogfight and not see a single German? I learned much later that phenomenon was not too uncommon. . . .

Later, in the 38th ready room, Wyche looked at me, quizzically, "What the hell happened back there?" he asked. "Why did you turn back?"

"I don't know," I replied, searching for an excuse. "I think I blacked out!"

"Blacked out?" he repeated. "Flying straight and level?"

66

"I guess I was mostly confused," I admitted.

Marvin Bledsoe, *P–47 pilot, 353rd Fighter Group (from* Thunderbolt*)*
Blick [Capt. Wayne Blickenstaff] motioned to me to tighten up the formation. I suspected he wanted to put on a show for the guys on the ground, so I tucked my wing in as close to his as I could. As we roared over the field, we were mere inches apart and less than six feet off the ground. We buzzed the runway, and I knew we were looking good. I stayed close as Blick made a sharp, sweeping turn and came in for a landing. My wheels touched the ground almost with his. We pulled off the runway together, and as I taxied off to my parking area Blick gave me the thumbs-up sign.

The ground crew ran out to meet me, waving and jumping up and down as I pulled into the revetment. I was their personal weapon against the Germans, and I made it back in one piece. The crew chief leaped up on the wing even before I had killed the motor. The prop was still turning over when he got the canopy open and pounded me on the back.

"Jeez, I'm glad to see you, lieutenant. We were really sweating you out. Our last pilot got knocked down on his first mission. God damn, but it sure looked good seeing you and the captain buzz the field in formation."

By now the other crew members had gathered around, congratulating me on coming back alive. They pumped my hand and patted me on the back. I felt like a hero.

This 357th Fighter Group P–51K was flown from Leiston by the 362nd Squadron's Jim Gasser. *Butch Baby* sits in the background. *Alexander C. Sloan via Bob Kuhnert, 355th FG Assn.*

Chapter 4

Overpaid, Oversexed and Over Here

Robert T. Sand, *propeller shop 55th Fighter Group*
September 6, 1943
Just had our first boat drill. On our way to "A" Deck we passed through some of the luxury parts of the ship. We were dumfounded, after experiencing the conditions we have lived under here. Beautiful halls, corridors and staterooms. A super lounge and dining room.

All this used by officers and nurses. We never saw such a lot of good looking girls in uniform. Most are usually rugged. The officers are clean and shaved, and allowed the company of the girls. These conditions are probably necessary, but it makes us feel like cattle—or as I heard a British officer describe it, "—running around like a bunch of bloody pigs!" Some of us now wish we had either gone to OCS [Officer Candidate School], or that we were women!
September 7, 1943
We had to go up on "A" deck while our deck was scrubbed today. Lots of officers and nurses. They had all the room in the world (until *we* arrived). They all looked so fresh and clean, the officers clean shaven, alongside us unshaven cattle.

Most of my gang had to go thirteen hours without going to a latrine, due to the strict traffic regulations on the boat. I've only been able to wash once since boarding. Haven't shaved. A few have shaved, showered and washed by breaking rules. Very few.

We are now in the compartment, stinking, hot and sweaty again. Have only eaten one meal in 48 hours, so maybe supper will go down tonight. Here it comes! . . . .

Chicken is just one of the meals served on china plates to officers and nurses, who were also officers. They even have a choice of menu, beautiful green upholstered chairs, fancy tables, etc.

There was a near mutiny, if noise means anything, by the men this morning, when the galley turned us down on seconds of anything.

September 13, 1943
On my way down to one of the galley store rooms to pick up a case of "C" rations, I saw several *tubs* full of steaks; beautiful, red, thick cuts, apparently for officers, as we had a sort of vegetable stew. It was fairly good at that. Cooked cabbage was the vegetable, as usual. Fooey!
September 1943
This morning began the pains of reassembling our personal equipment. Then the stealing which had already been rampant this whole voyage turned into the worst outrage of mass thievery I have ever seen. Barracks bags, bedrolls, guns, clothing, *everything*, stolen left and right. Some things were recovered, many things not. Someone got Rod's [Fraleigh] gas mask, and while I was standing right by it, someone stole my breakfast "C" ration for tomorrow. I also lost a hand towel. Recovered my spoon and fork, used and dirty, that was taken from my kit the first day. Also my soap dish, the soap used. Everywhere there are messkits lying about, which had

4th Fighter Group ace Don Gentile engages in a fighter pilot's favorite
pastime. *USAF/NASM*

been used once, then thrown aside, and someone else's used.

Jack Monaghan, *maintenance supply, 55th Fighter Group*

When we landed in Greenock, Scotland, we learned an interesting British regulation. I am not sure if this is still true but at that time no foreigner could land on British shores carrying any arms or ammunition. As we came off the troop transport, the *Orion*, a British ship, we had to hand over our arms and ammunition to someone aboard ship before we went down the gangplank to the dock. The guns and ammunition were collected on the deck, were lowered over the side to another British vessel and brought to shore and handed back to us again so that no foreigner carried arms and ammunition onto British shores. We had to identify our weapons by serial number when they returned our arms.

Robert T. Sand, *propeller shop, 55th Fighter Group*

When the Group arrived at Nuthampstead, England, in September of 1943, the weather was already turning cold and soggy. Like most wartime airfields, this one was hastily constructed by the English and widely dispersed on farmland, connected by existing country roads. For living quarters, we enlisted men were assigned to a small area consisting of about four Nissen huts for barracks, one Nissen hut for an orderly room, a latrine a dozen yards from the huts. They were shelter indeed, which front line infantry would have considered palatial, I am sure. It is also true that they were bare, uninsulated metal, drafty and dimly lit. Small wattage bulbs were used to conserve scarce energy, and there was always a shortage of fuel for the tiny stove that tried unsuccessfully to heat the frigid air that lay over England for most of

those two years. Usually a sea of gumbo mud surrounded these buildings. The barracks were connected by sidewalks, but the latrine was not. It was a challenge to make the crossing without having your boots sucked into the gumbo and sometimes the trip was too urgent to stop and retrieve them.

The showers were separate little buildings quite some distance from the barracks area. The stories coming back to us about the showers filled us with foreboding, but the time soon came when a shower was essential.

This is what we found: The time of day left for showers was after work, and after chow, so the trip to the shower building was a long walk through blackness, with the careful flicking on and off of a penlight to stay on sidewalk or road. From out of the cold dark night we entered a room nearly as dark. Steam swirled out of the open door and was torn away by

Huddled into Hut 16 at Nuthampstead, Technical Sergeant Hoch writes home, 28 March 1944. *Robert T. Sand*

70

Wormingford, 12 May 1944. Red Cross doughnut girls were loved by almost everyone who came in contact with them. They were always ready with a smile, an encouraging word and the simple presence of a woman in a man's world. *Robert T. Sand*

the night breeze. The inside had shower heads, not stalls, arrayed along one or two sides of the room. The rest of the room contained rows of benches for changing clothes. These were made of 1″x1″ slats, as were the floor sections which were now floating in confusion on three or four inches of dirty, soapy water, on which also floated soggy cigarette butts and all manners of paper scraps. All drains were plugged.

Home for 55th Fighter Group ground crewman Sgt. Bob Sand, who slept in the top bunk of this cot at Wormingford. *Robert T. Sand*

Just below the prop maintenance shops at Wormingford sat this windmill, built in that late 1700s. England at war was a nation of contrasts. *Robert T. Sand*

We did as the others were doing, climbed on the benches and commenced a balancing act of removing clothing, rolling it into a ball and stashing it with the shoes on the driest part of the bench. Stowed the clean long handled underwear the same way, hoping it would not fall into the soup. Same with the towel. We reluctantly stepped down on the skittery floating platforms and sloshed our way to the shower heads, barely visible in the dim, steamy light. Here, men were shrieking. One because his shower was dispensing ice cold water, and the one next to him because his was scalding hot. They tried running back and forth to temper the pain a bit. I found one which was all plugged up except for a couple of holes which sent out a needle spray of very hot water.

When the installers had finished the plumbing, all handles were removed from the heat controls, supposedly to conserve hot water. Mechanics soon learned to bring pliers when they showered.

Anyway, the struggle with soap, washcloth, towel, and the balancing act of trying to dress atop the by now soggy benches, without dropping things in the water, was epic and unforgettable. Over the months these conditions gradually improved, but it was little solace when we knew the officers were bathing in Roman tiled sunken baths smothered in bubbles and listening to Vera Lynn singing the latest songs while beautiful houris adjusted the water temperature with solid gold knobs and scraped their skin with whalebone after anointing them with oil.

Well, I have to admit that the part about the officers came through the grapevine and may differ in some details, but I can attest to every word of the enlisted men's experience firsthand.

Marvin Bledsoe, *P-47 pilot, 353rd Fighter Group (from* Thunderbolt*)*

It was always dark when we got up. It was invariably wet with fog outside our Nissen huts, and cold as cold could be inside or out. Night and day the English air chilled me to the bone. Right after my arrival, I wrote and asked [my wife] Harriet to make a flannel sleeping outfit for me with feet, mittens and a hood for my head. She added rabbit ears to the hood, and I was teased unmercifully about my "bunny suit." But from then on I slept warmly.

Chet A. Patterson, *P-38 pilot, 55th Fighter Group*

The 338th Squadron had reserved a room in one of the nicer hotels in London. It had two bedrooms and a sitting room. As each flight went in for their R&R the room just kept rotating with the flights.

Once as four men were getting into an elevator a young, very attractive lady got in with them. Immediately each man tuned in hoping for a date for the evening. She seemed very pleased with the attention. As the elevator stopped at her floor, the men almost said in unison, "Would you like to come up to our room for a drink?"

She said, "Yes," and as far as the pilots were concerned the chase was on. When she got to the room each man was jockeying for position. It seems her father was in the Parliament and she had studied to be a ballet dancer before the war started.

Somehow the conversation got into ballet dancing and she was asked to show a couple of movements. She accepted the challenge.

In trying to demonstrate, she decided she had to shed her heavy clothes. So, in bra and panties, she gave the pilots a demonstration and I don't think they ever saw any of the dance steps. An outsider watching this would wonder who was the "chassee" and who was the "chaser."

She pointed to one of the pilots, said, "Follow me," and headed for one of the bedrooms. That left three broken hearts wondering why they were not chosen. Not too long after that the door opened and she came out to choose another pilot while the first man crashed on the sofa. This was repeated till all four were shot down.

So for the next two days of leave no one left the room and the woman should have but didn't get her fill of young, eager pilots. When they left they asked her to stay for the next flight that would be following them.

This went on for several flights. I felt something was wrong with the way the fellows were returning after their leaves. The normal was a few hangovers with attached headaches, somewhat depressed because the leave wasn't long enough, etc. Everyone seemed to have a big smile and no hangovers. I asked Dr. Randy Garnett to check up on what was going on.

He came back to tell me what was happening at the hotel. As soon as I heard I got a car and along with Dr. Garnett we headed for London. In my mind if she was a German agent she could put the 338th Squadron out of business if she had a social disease. I wanted Dr. Garnett to check her right away and he was a GYN so this was right down his line.

Dr. Garnett gave her a clean bill of health and said she was a nymphomaniac. In the taxi taking her back to the hotel we told her to let us know if she ever went outside the squadron. Otherwise she was free to stay in the room and I was sure the men would bring her special treats.

This went on for over a month and then one day she just disappeared. I knew something changed for the next flight came back with bo-que headaches, assorted hangovers and obvious signs of depression.

Robert T. Sand, *Propeller shop, 55th Fighter Group*

The second Christmas passed as another workday for us, but spirits weren't too low. We had a pretty good turkey dinner Christmas Day. Christmas Eve was a milling, informal party, or parties, in all the huts and we

On the six-mile stretch of road from Colchester to the 55th field at Wormingford sat this old flour mill, a constant reminder of changing times. *Robert T. Sand*

had quite a lot of beer and spirits, and snacks assembled from packages from home. I got a little tight, but not like last year.

Even got to decorate a Christmas tree this year (for the day room). Christmas paper stuffed with balls of newspaper and tied with ribbons made decorations, also a blue cellophane bow, a few little Santas robbed from another home-sent tree, and a few salvaged icicles. The tree is about five feet tall and sits on a table. Surgical cotton serves as a snow base, and snow patches on tree, and shredded radar f.u. (foul up) tinfoil for sparkles. Our communications officer donated us a string of lights made up of gunsight bulbs, painted, but it didn't burn very brightly, and soon burned out. With another soldier I helped cut some red berries on a side road and some holly at the nearby minister's estate, and with the leftover limbs of the Xmas tree, we did a pretty nice job of decorating the day room. We

used the radar tinfoil about the same as you use colored straws by tying bunches of it to form pretty flared out disks.

Arthur L. Thorsen, *P-38 pilot, 55th Fighter Group*

We were assigned to various shacks and issued three iron hard pillows, to be used as a mattress. We called them biscuits. We also received blankets made, it seemed, of steel wool and thorns. I was gradually beginning to feel better instead of worse, for I reasoned that if I were eventually shot down and taken prisoner, prison camp couldn't possibly be a greater hardship than this.

Chet A. Patterson, *P-38 pilot, 55th Fighter Group*

There were some billets on Wormingford called the VIP quarters. It housed some 20 or 25 men and was a Quonset hut built in the form of a T.

The horizontal bar of the T was the largest portion and had the rooms. The vertical shape was much smaller and contained the showers, johns and washstands. There were four large rooms for two on the corners while the rest of the rooms were small individual units. Dr. Randy Garnett and I were roommates and had been close personal friends since the days of Port Angeles.

We had a dance held in the Officer's Club when they invited English girls from the Land Army to the party. The weather was bad and forecast for getting worse so you might say it was a "maximum effort" for all the officers. There were no holds barred for they knew they could sleep in the next day.

I don't know how many scored in this encounter but two men in the VIP quarters ended up with girls in their room. Obviously it was a mutual attraction for both sexes and they did what came naturally. In the wee hours

There was nothing more popular than Bob Hope's touring USO show which made its way across the globe through all theaters of war. As Bob Sand recalled, "Bob Hope's pin-up girls got more attention from GIs than Bob Hope . . . gee, they looked good!" *Robert T. Sand*

An ironmonger's wagon passing through Colchester seems out of place when compared to the modern fighter ironmongery on nearby airfields. *Robert T. Sand*

London's Piccadilly Circus in 1945 was a constant magnet for Yanks on leave. *Byron Trent*

of the morning one of the girls had to go to the john. Her partner told her to just leave the door ajar and feel her way down the hall, turn left and then left again at the next opening. Naturally she was to return the same as we had a very strict blackout. Only the john area had a dim light.

I guess this noise of her leaving the room also caused the other girl to decide to do the same thing and she happened to be in the next room. She got the same instructions, however this room was closest to the john. Now there [were] two doors left ajar so when the first girl got back she entered the first room and closed the door. The second girl did the same thing. As long as both couples were awake (the beds were single cots) they again did what came naturally. Mind you they all had met for the first time and with a little liquor to dim their senses no one noticed any difference.

When dawn came and there was sufficient light, one of the girls awoke to look into a face of a total stranger. She let out a wild yell and this woke everyone in the building (soundproofing was not a requirement for these buildings).

Randy and I jumped up and ran to the rooms. One of the cardinal rules was no rough stuff at any time. By the time we got there the second gal awoke with the shout and she too was screaming. The two pilots were totally confused. Fortunately, though the women accused the men of switching, of course the pilots were each in their own room.

After separating the pilots and the women we finally figured out what happened. It was hard not to laugh right then but it was still a bitter experience to the women. We had

them gather their clothes and had them taken home by the squadron jeep.

Robert T. Sand, *P-51 ground crew, 55th Fighter Group*

I live in a Nissen hut, which is the British prototype of a Pacific hut. We have a little coal stove, but still, they aren't exactly warm, and the wind leaks through. Have an iron cot, with a three section mattress of unresisting material. I sleep on the mattress and over me are two American Army blankets, two gray British blankets (one folded double to give an extra layer), my overcoat, my Mackinaw, and sometimes my sweater and leather sheep jacket. No sheets. The wool tickles one's face all night. The pillow is a round cylinder of horsehair and dried camel dung (well, maybe not) and is covered by a coarse, sack-like slip. I removed over half its stuffing, and it's not bad now.

In spite of the fact that this sack (bed) is bringing back my old rheumatism, I am always reluctant to leave it in the morning.

Jan Houston Monaghan, *Red Cross girl, 55th Fighter Group*

The base at Wormingford was overrun with dogs . . . all kinds: big ones, little ones, with long legs, short legs, long tails, no tails, cute and cuddly and ugly as sin. They would come into the Red Cross Club and climb up in the chairs to sleep. Most of the time they were filthy and made the upholstery, such as it was, filthy too. The men thought I was a mean gal because I would go through the club and tip the chairs to make the

dogs fall out and then I shooed them outside. The fellows didn't seem to mind giving up chairs to dogs, but I thought that was ridiculous. Whenever an announcement was made over the Tannoy [public address system] to the effect, "All dogs that are not registered will be put to sleep," every guy would hasten to adopt a dog and have it registered. The dog population grew and grew and I fought a losing battle with the chairs.

Robert T. Sand, *Propeller shop, 55th Fighter Group*

It may sound funny, but the byword over here is "It's *rough* in the ETO!" Fact is, mister, when the ETO G.I. reads of your troubles back home, he just laughs. Income tax? "Boy, ain't that tough!" he chuckles. Rationing? "It'd be a pleasure!" he says. Prices? Well, Uncle Sam takes care of our clothing account pretty well, though the styles are rather limited. But I've heard of G.I.s paying as much as twenty-five shillings for one dozen eggs, and mister, that is more than five good old American dollars. Ninety cents a dozen is a more common price in the country, *if* you *know* someone, and are very *lucky*. Try and get them!

Rationing, eh? No whipping cream over there? Hm! Well, there's none over here either, or commercial cream . . . or milk! Condensed milk is used for our coffee, powdered milk for the cereal. We don't complain . . . but! Our favorite food back home, ice cream, is a very rare thing over here, and cannot be obtained in public at all. When we do get it in the mess hall, it tastes like canned milk, but we consider it a gala occasion.

We don't have butter at every meal, and about half the butter (by my guess) has been canned butter, with a large percentage of cottonseed oil to help it withstand warm temperatures. It does! It refuses to spread on anything. Won't melt on hot foods, and it leaves a coating in one's mouth that is very unpleasant. We've learned to pass it up if we recognize it though the day may come when we'll be glad to get it.

Have you ever heard of "C" rations, mister? Ever tasted 'em? Well,

it's a sort of finely chopped hash, with a certain taste and feeling in your mouth. Ask any G.I. who has lived over here what he thinks of them! Oh! for a good, cold bowl of crackers and milk!

[Breakfast] comes this way to a G.I. . . .

He is awakened by the C.Q. (charge of quarters) at a plenty early hour, and after battling with his apprehension of the icy air outside his

finally warmed pile of blankets, overcoats, jackets, sweaters, overalls, etc., he drags himself out and pulls on the layers of shapeless clothing that characterize the Army mechanic. Then, if he remembers his childhood training, he sloshes his way to the almost deserted wash-house to dash some ice water (there is only one kind) into his face, a quick towel rub with cold, numbed hands, a few hurried strokes of the toothbrush, and

Local pubs became very popular, very quickly. These GIs from the 355th Fighter Group are clearly enjoying the ancient English tradition of paying one's respects to the local publican and his wife by having a pint. *Alexander C. Sloan via Bob Kuhnert, 355th FG Assn.*

then back to the hut to make up the sack (they just *aren't* beds over here) and sweep up a bit. Finally, with an envious look at the few G.I.s fortunate enough to be able to sleep in, he grabs the ever-present messkit and goes out into the darkness towards the mess hall.

The road is narrow, and a dozen times he has to step off onto the slippery, muddy shoulder, averting his head to try ineffectually to shield his face from the fine shower of mud as Army vehicles hurtle past.

A few minutes' walk and he reaches the mess hall, only to find that the chowline extends from fifty to a hundred yards outside the door. So, he stands with his back to the wind, and tucks his mess gear into his jacket to warm it up a little from the heat that is in his body, if any.

And here is one of the evils of the Army . . . "Sweating out the chowline." What a long-gone dream, that—the days we used to only walk into the next room to find bright china plates, and shiny silverware on a clean, white table! Most G.I.s would trade you all your troubles for just that!

Anyway, the shivering G.I. hunches up in his jacket, and moving one step at a time, sometimes stopping for a while, he gradually moves toward his first goal, which is the shelter of the doorway. Once inside, he starts the juggling act of removing his gloves and cap, stuffing them into pockets, trying to untie the messkit bag, and unsnap the handle of the canteen cup before the line passes the fruit juice, which is placed near the door. Gulping the juice down so he will have the cup ready for coffee, he unsnaps the messkit, which sometimes

requires a sharp bang on the table, causing the messkit to open with such explosive force everyone in the chowline jumps. And there isn't a chowline in which at least one messkit doesn't slip from someone's grasp and explode with a clatter of dancing knives, forks, etc., across the floor.

With practiced motions, the G.I. pokes knife, fork and spoon into a pocket, balances messkit and messkit lid in the fingers of the left hand, tucks the cup under the left arm, and is finally ready to serve himself. If something special is on the menu, such as real eggs, the cooks wisely do not trust the individual to serve himself. The food is in large containers placed on a counter some fifteen feet long, and the line splits, forming a line on each side of the counter.

Let's see, what does the G.I. have for breakfast this morning? It's an unusually good one, and there is more variety than usual. Pancakes! Happy Day! The rightfully *un*happy K.P. flops two pancakes onto the G.I.'s proffered messkit lid. Next he helps himself to a ladle of syrup. Then with a long, two-tined fork, he chases a piece or two of bacon floating in three inches of melted fat. Since the man on the other side is doing the same thing, it practically amounts to a duel. After a minute or two of exasperating effort he decides he didn't want any bacon anyway. It looks a lot different than the home kind variety, too.

Next is the cold cereal. It looks something like the old familiar Wheaties we once knew, but upon the application of milk it instantly assumes all the properties of a soggy pulp. Nor does it seem to be "flavored with additional salt and malt extract,"

because it is quite tasteless. Then comes the milk, which he ladles out steaming hot, with a surface foam, and many little powder-lumps which look like rice on the surface of the cereal.

Now things are getting tricky, especially if yours is the old model messkit with the shallow lid. You can't keep lid and kit on the same level, and you are either spilling syrup from one or milk from the other. There is even fruit this morning. Cooked, dried apricots. Now where to put 'em? Oh, well, they look as tough as leather, and your mouth puckers just thinking how sour they are. Let's skip 'em.

There is almost always butter with hotcakes, so again he does the chasing act with a two pronged fork, trying to capture elusive cubes of butter floating in a pan of water. O.K. Now he no longer needs his right hand, so he retrieves the cup from under his arm, and a K.P. fills it with coffee.

Balancing is at a critical stage, now. Hold your finger on the cup-handle latch, because if it slips out it will dump the entire contents on the floor so quickly you never fail to be astonished, and worse. He half squats to get the cup under the condensed milk spout, and the K.P. gives it a quick squirt. With his other hand the K.P. tosses an enormous slab of light brown bread onto the kit, or cup, if you want it at all, and the G.I. is ready to eat.

Well, not quite. Getting a place to sit is another matter. He looks up and down the long line of tables and finally spots a place only about five men from the outside end of the table. With his heart in his mouth, he carefully steps out in that direction, trying to make shoulders and arms glide smoothly, and trying to avoid the bumping of the constant streams of heavy traffic.

Squeezing in between two rows of leather clad backs he gingerly sidesteps towards his goal, hoping no one decides suddenly to stand up, and hoping that if someone does, he's a smaller guy than himself.

Ah! Now, he sets his cup down, pushes aside the crusts of bread left by the last three men, and contemplates what to do about the ever present puddle of milk or fruit juice in the middle of the space. Finally, he sets his gear as much to one side of it as possible and then climbs awkwardly over the bench, knocking his neighbor's elbows with his knees as he does so.

Meanwhile the aluminum messkit is draining the heat from the food with alarming rapidity. The food is seldom very hot in the first place, as it must be cooked hours ahead of time, and kept in the large pots and pans until serving time. Only very recently has our own shift of cooks provided a can of warm water at the head of the serving line, for taking the outdoor's chill from the messgear . . . this helps considerably.

Now, he is ready to eat. He pleads above the noise for the sugar (yes, we still have sugar, very coarse, but plenty good enough). It finally reaches him, and usually his worst fears are realized . . . it is what is commonly known in G.I. circles as "cinched." This means that if he uses any of it, it's a darn cinch that the next one to use it will have to refill it, so according to Army courtesy, he is bound to forestall this tragedy by filling the sugar tin himself. Complicated, but customary. The movements about the table of such table-supplied foods are as strategically planned [as] a game of chess, each man craftily trying to avoid being the recipient of a "cinch."

But, the G.I. has it, so he struggles out of his seat, picks up the little sugar tin and beats his way to the sugar barrel for a refill. When he gets back, his food is only lukewarm, so he gulps it down as fast as possible before it gets completely cold.

Just eating is quite a job. Since you have on your bulky clothing (sheepskin jacket, and sometimes sheepskin pants) you find that every movement of your arms tends to knock utensils one way or another, and your scarf keeps trying to trail in the food. When you raise a spoonful of food to your mouth, the stiff jacket goes up with it so that the collar blocks the way. You try tucking it in different ways, but finally end up holding it down with your left hand.

A welcome final destination on leave—the American Red Cross Service Club at the Bull Hotel, Cambridge. *Alexander C. Sloan via Bob Kuhnert, 355th FG Assn.*

Rainbow Corner, the American Red Cross Club on Shaftsbury Avenue, just off Piccadilly Circus in London. *Alexander C. Sloan via Bob Kuhnert, 355th FG Assn.*

Finally the G.I. drinks his coffee, which doesn't taste like the old homemade coffee, then he threads lid, knife, fork and spoon onto the messkit handle, and heads for the steamy washing room. After emptying scraps into a garbage can, he gets into one of the lines, each leading to three huge kettles, beneath which smoky coal fires are burning. The first is soapy water (except when we run out of soap), the second contains disinfectant, and the third a final rinse in hot water. All goes well here except when the meal is of a greasy nature, or the water is not hot, or there is no soap, or you drop part of your gear into one of the deep kettles.

Then, slipping and sliding in the mud, the ETO soldier goes around to the front of the messhall, meanwhile assembling mess gear, cap, gloves, etc., and joins the crowd waiting for the chowtruck—"bus" to you. Everyone tries to find some shelter in the lee of the little Nissen shack, but there isn't room for everyone, and shoes pick up heavy gumbo with every step.

Just like any bus back home, it seems that fate decrees that the bus must pull out just the moment before you get there. So, everyone huddles and waits. There is horseplay and talk. I know how crowded busses are at home, but you should see ours! The moment our particular truck comes into sight with a clattering roar of the exhaust, there is a mad rush towards it long before it stops, and a seething battle to get on it. The mob bails into the back of the truck, which is equipped with some steps made by our shop, and in the wink of an eye, the benches lining each side are filled and G.I.s are sitting on other G.I.s'

laps, and then every available inch of standing space, leaning space, squatting space, is taken up and then some more are crowded on. For a time we used a truck designed to carry eighteen men, and we've counted as many as forty-four coming out of it. Now we use a roomier truck, but still just as proportionately packed. Until MP law clamped down recently the steps and tail gate were loaded in a swaying bulge of humanity hanging on for dear life.

There are no upholstered seats in these busses, no windows, and no light when crowded. If you are toward the front, all you can see are faintly dimmed, disconnected parts of human beings . . . a nose, a jaw, a hand, someone's back, a foot. The driver is an unmerciful guy with a mania for making his cargo as uncomfortable as possible by starting fast, stopping fast and swinging fast around the curves. The mob swings and sways, desperately trying to maintain balance by grasping anything possible, even a neighbor, whose own balance is equally precarious. Sometimes you are shocked to find that a bodyless head is protruding from between your knees, or that a foot has found its way into your lap.

If you happen to be sitting anywhere near the back of the truck, you are favored by a fine spray of mud that clouds glasses, and leaves one whole side of you a glistening coat of brown mud. In spite of this, it is all endured in a spirit of good humor, and most complaints are good-natured.

The thing is, this whole procedure is repeated with little change, except for menu, and weather conditions, three times a day, day in and day out.

It has lost its novelty, if it ever had any.

Jan Houston Monaghan, *Red Cross girl, 55th Fighter Group*
On July 6, 1944, one month after D-day, I arrived on the base at Wormingford and met Nelle Huse with whom I would work for the next seventeen months. After I unpacked, Nelle took me to the Aero Club and introduced me to the British staff, showed me around and described my particular responsibilities as Program Director. When we went back to our quarters, I asked, "What do we do now?"

"Well," Nelle said, in her soft southern drawl, "the girl who was here before you always went to the Officers' Club for cocktails before dinner."

"Is that what you do? Do we have to?" I wanted to know.

"No, I don't go because I don't drink," Nelle replied.

"You don't? Neither do I!" I exclaimed, delighted to find a non-drinking buddy and so cocktails at the Officers' Club never became a part of our daily routine. We ate our meals there, helped to decorate the club for their dances and always attended since dancing partners were needed, but most of our time was spent with the enlisted men. The Officers had their club and the Red Cross Aero Club provided a place for the enlisted personnel to meet.

Nelle was everyone's love and her beautiful photogenic smile had won her distinction as one of the beauties at the University of Alabama. She married Lt. John Huse, a West Point graduate, in 1940 when he was at Lackland Field, San Antonio,

Texas. John was in the Philippines at the time of Pearl Harbor and was shot down over Java in early 1942.

"One day in our Red Cross office someone mentioned an article in a recent paper about a flyer being found alive in a jungle when he had been presumed dead. A wistful expression crossed Nelle's face prompting me to ask, 'You wish that could be your John, don't you, Nelle?'

"'Yes,' she said sadly, 'but it's impossible because the other men in his outfit saw John crash and they buried him there in Java. I had letters from his commanding officer and others telling me all about it.'"
Robert T. Sand, *Propeller shop, 55th Fighter Group*

August 3, 1944 was one of those rare, beautiful autumn days, and little

The wheat field behind the work line at Wormingford the day after the GI shocking of August 3, 1944. *Robert T. Sand*

82

work to do. A small crew of English farmers showed up and began shocking the turned and dried rows of wheat. Gradually, G.I.s drifted over to the fence to watch. Many were ex-farm workers, and watched longingly as the few men made slow progress on the big field, and talked nostalgically of harvests they remembered. Suddenly one man could stand it no longer, jumped the fence, and plunged into the work, setting an example of speed and enthusiasm that must have astonished the English men.

This was too much for the watching G.I.s and, as if obeying a World War I order to "go over the top," a whole army of frustrated farmers leaped over the fence and soon covered the entire field, with arms flailing, everyone competing to tie and stack faster than the others. It was a fantastic scene. I always wondered what the English farmers thought as they saw this wild horde advancing pell-mell across their field towards them and demanding binding twine. That entire field was shocked so fast it was unbelievable, and a happier crew you never saw.

Jan Houston Monaghan, *Red Cross girl, 55th Fighter Group*

The living quarters for the Red Cross girls were at the end of the Commissary building where the rats spent the day gorging themselves and then, at night, came down to our end and played tag. They slid down the Nissen Hut roof, squealing and scampering until they woke us up at night. Nelle would get so mad she threw her shoes at the sloping ceiling.

The rats gnawed holes along the baseboard about which we complained about to the English maintenance crew. They simply said, "No use patching the holes, they'll only make more."

We covered the holes with stacks of bricks, some stacks were two feet high. Once a rat died on a nest of babies in the wall behind the bathtub. The smell of dead rats became so overpowering, we had to give up taking baths until someone could come, move the tub, make a hole in the wall and remove the nest. Another rat died behind one of our brick piles in the guest room. I was away on leave and when I returned, I asked Nelle if she'd had the rat taken away.

"Oh, yes," she replied, casually, "I did it myself. I just took a couple of sticks, lifted up the rat and carried it to the garbage bin." Dainty little Nelle continually amazed me.

Gilbert C. Burns, Jr, *P-47 pilot, Fighter OTU*

On July 16, 1944, I took off from the OTU at Atcham, England with no particular objective in mind. The razorback P-47 was 41–6237, an old one, one of the first few hundred made at Farmingdale, New York. Its cost then was about $85,000. When a fighter pilot flies, he is supposed to keep his head turning, constantly watching in all directions. The reason, of course, being that no enemy aircraft could approach and catch you by surprise.

I was flying in the vicinity of Shrewsbury and my mind was not on flying, but on other things. I was not looking around, but staring straight ahead. I had "my head up my ass." I happened to turn my head to the left and lo and behold, what was sitting close to my left wing but a Spitfire. It had come up and caught me unawares. I was quite embarrassed and I am sure the Spitfire pilot was quite pleased about it. I took a close look at the pilot and there was blond hair coming down from beneath a white flying helmet. A girl! One of the English ATA ferry pilots. I knew that those girls were great pilots. I had seen them slow roll on take-off from our airfield. I had seen them in Hurricanes fly across our field only a few hundred feet up and inverted.

So this blonde ATA pilot must have felt pretty proud after catching me asleep at the wheel, and she dove off down to the left. Being more than annoyed with myself, I jumped on her tail and followed her down. She led a merry chase on the deck, but I clung to her. We were circling a huge tree in a vertical bank when suddenly my engine stopped. I glanced at the fuel gauges; they checked out OK, so with what power I had left, I pulled up a few hundred feet to look for a crash landing site. God was with me because there was a field off to the left and in I went. I turned off the ignition, shut the gas line off, put the flaps down, wheels up, trying to come in as slowly as possible.

I hit the ground tail first and crash-slid to a stop. Releasing my oxygen connection, radio cable and safety belt, I jumped out and started running in case the plane decided to blow. I looked back over my shoulder at the plane while I was running and what was chasing me but a bull! I kept running and came to a barbed wire fence that surrounded the field. With the bull coming up fast, I jumped over the fence. Going over the barbs ripped the seat of my flying suit and drew blood on my behind. This was to be my only "wound" of the war.

A jeep was sent for me finally and I returned to base. After telling my CO the story I asked him, in jest, if that "wound" would qualify me for a Purple Heart. He quickly informed me that they did not give medals for chasing blondes.

Jan Houston Monaghan, *Red Cross girl, 55th Fighter Group*

Christmas Day 1944 was one day none of us will forget. The weather had been 'socked in' for days and the planes had been unable to give air support to the Battle of the Bulge, but Christmas morning dawned clear, cold and bright. The sky was filled with planes from one horizon to the other, in layers as high as the eye could see. Everything in England that could fly was in the air that day heading for the continent.

As I stood staring at the spectacle, I found myself praying, "Oh God, it's Christmas . . . watch over those at the other end . . . and help us find peace someday. . . ."

A few years later I mentioned that Christmas at a meeting and a young woman in the group said, "I remember that Christmas too . . . I was at the other end. . . ."

Robert T. Sand, *Propeller shop, 55th Fighter Group*

I got my first view of an air raid from the target itself. Have seen others, but never before from the middle. It was indeed a rather awesome spectacle. But more than anything, I was impressed by the people themselves. The shows had just let out, and the already thronged streets were mobbed, when the wailing sirens shrieked out the

English farmhouses such as this one were not primarily something of historical interest to GIs. Here a USAAF officer and his enlisted driver are on a serious mission in the East Anglian countryside—hunting and bartering for fresh eggs. *Mark H. Brown/USAFA*

84

familiar rising and falling tone that is "red alert." Did people head for the shelter and undergrounds? Did the double-deck buses, the taxis stop, or turn out their lights? Or were traffic lights turned off? Hell, no! Everything went on its merry way; the people crowding and laughing in utter disregard for any danger from above.

At first there were a few flickers on the horizon, then they gradually grew closer, until you could hear the whoom! whoom! of the concussions. I can't tell at a distance the difference between bombs and anti-aircraft guns. Only when searchlights broke out right around us did the streets begin to clear somewhat of pedestrians. The noise and flashes grew greater and greater till it was for all the world like a terrific thunderstorm. Then all of a sudden there was a violent "bloom-bloom-bloom!" from an anti-aircraft battery right near us. A couple of feet from me I heard one girl say to her girlfriend, "I'm *scared*, aren't you?" The other answered, "Yes," and they said little more. And other girls and guys barged back and forth, laughing and talking. The buses kept plugging along. I was part of quite a crowd of curious gathered in a semi-sheltered place where we could see everything well.

A tall, respectable-looking gent leaned down and kissed his wife and said, "Don't worry, dear, it's all right."

We couldn't see the planes, but we could follow their course by the pin-pricks of light, high overhead, that spelled death, and we could sometimes hear the engines. It passed on to a moderate distance, growing muffled. Some of the people passed on, but I stayed to see it all. Soon the barrage grew closer, and was right on

us again, and new people were standing by me. A tall, middle-aged woman was standing near, and I decided she wasn't young enough to think I was trying to proposition her if I spoke to her.

"This beats me. If anything like this occurred back home, there wouldn't be a soul on the street, or a light, or a vehicle running."

The conversation continued about like this. (Meanwhile, my knees were doing a jitterbug number.)

The lady: "Well (boomety-boom-boom!) we've grown so used (boom, boom, boom!) so used to it, you (boom-bloom!) see."

Me (or I—one of us, anyway): "Yes, but how can anyone get so used to it that it doesn't bother them? After all (boom!) that's a lot of high-power stuff going off, and with the shrapnel falling and all?"

The lady: "Yes, but they know when it is bad enough to head for shelter. They don't like shelters. They are afraid of indirect hits, and of being trapped. You are safer in the open. I usually watch this from my hotel roof, but the lift isn't running right now."

For the third time the bombers are coming back. The sky is a constant blaze of flashes. The din is terrific. The lady watches unperturbed: "They seem to (boom, boom, boom!) be coming back (wham! bloom!) again. This is a (blam! Wham blam!) this is a rather (Whoom!) a small (wham, blam, boom!) a small affair tonite."

I faint! Mentally, anyway.

However, when I got back here, one or two of the porters (or janitors) had been watching it from the roof, and seemed to have quite a bit of

news to report, but I couldn't get close enough to hear it.

Tomorrow the paper will say, if anything, "Enemy aircraft were over London last night. One old lady in a nursing home was killed. Some anti-aircraft firing was heard."

Radio news says fifty bombers reached the outskirts of London, but only ten penetrated to the center. Six reported shot down so far. Pfui! Only ten bombers! What is ten or fifteen tons of bombs? Pfui! I still say it is much.

Arthur L. Thorsen, *P–38 pilot, 55th Fighter Group*
[During a London air raid] someone shouted, "Let's get down in the bloody cellar where the bloody wine is kept!" There was no panic. The party guests, mostly English, were used to this sort of thing and slipped out of the [hotel] suite in small groups. Those raids were nothing compared to the blitz of 1940 and '41, and only occurred with lengthy intervals between.

The door to one of the bedrooms slammed open and Penn came out with only one pant leg on. Staggering around, trying to get his other leg into his pants, he said, "Those goddam Jerries! Their timing is always rotten." Ethel followed him out of the bedroom, buttoning her blouse.

"Nice party," she said, "Where's Jackie?"

"Went out with the others." I replied. "She might have gone to the cellar."

"Not Jackie," said Ethel, "she's a queer one. Likes to watch the raids. She's probably out in front of the hotel."

Woods, Jaklich, and DesVoignes were gathering up the remaining bottles. "Let's go watch the show with Jackie," suggested Jaklich. We all agreed that was a good idea and left the suite. The only person left behind was correspondent Leatherby, asleep in a corner, in a drunken stupor.

By the time we reached street level, the first bombers were coming over, some getting caught in searchlights. Then the anti-aircraft opened up and the sky came alive with orange flashes. The bombers were hitting the dock area at the Victoria embankment again. One bomb seemed very close, hitting a building on Bedford Street to our right. It did a half roll in the air.

Not all of the party went to the shelters. Some of the RAF fliers and their girlfriends had joined us on the curb. We all sat there, enjoying the show the same as folks back home would enjoy a fireworks display. We began passing the bottles around as

pieces of shell casings fell to the street with loud clatters. The whole exercise seemed to be a variation on the "chicken" game. Everyone sweated their way through it, none wanting to be the first "chicken" to run for a shelter. In about ten minutes the "all clear" sounded and we went back to the suite. No one else returned, so the party broke up. . . .

I wasn't really tired and did not go directly to my room. Instead, I took the elevator down to the ground floor and stepped out into the night. There was a red glow in the sky over the docks and another over Bedford Street. Curious, I walked down the Strand toward Bedford. Turning the corner, I could see the bombed building burning and being attended to by firefighters. As I approached, ambulances went racing back and forth. Some civilians were standing in groups on the periphery of the burning building, and, noticing one gentleman standing alone, I stepped to his side.

He was well dressed with bowler hat and umbrella and he was cursing quietly to himself.

"Did everyone get out?" I asked.

"Very few," he replied, "and they're in pretty bad shape. This was a WAAF barracks. Women's Auxiliary Air Force, you know. They manage the barrage balloon in Victoria Gardens."

"Can we help?"

"'fraid not. We'd only be in the way. Those chaps know their business better than we. There's not much left of the ladies, I'm afraid. Look there!" and he pointed with his umbrella to an object lying in the glow of the fire. I saw what appeared to be a bloody human spine.

Robert T. Sand, *propeller shop, 55th Fighter Group*

As far as I know, there were no bomb shelters [at the time] at Nuthampstead. Certainly none in our barracks area. Almost right away we

The Orderly Room crew at Nuthampstead, the 55th Fighter Group's first base, December 1943. Mud was a constant in England, getting into everything imaginable and miring down even the most elaborate anti-gumbo devices. Corporal Horn snaps Captain Boggess' picture as (right to left): Sergeant Laque, Sergeant Fladung, Staff Sergeant Golden and Corporal Anderson look on. *Robert T. Sand*

The 55th Group mess hall during lunch at Wormingford, 7 May 1944. Upper non-coms were issued bikes but the lower-ranking enlisted men had to buy theirs. *Robert T. Sand*

began to wonder if it wouldn't be nice to have some. Most histories I have read of WWII in Britain say there were no significant air raids by the Germans over England after the Blitz. It would have been hard to convince us of that fact in Nuthampstead in late 1943 or early 1944.

One night we were awakened by a series of explosions that seemed mighty close. Our instructions in case of an air raid were to crawl under our cots until it was over. Very few did so, whether out of bravado, or futility, I don't know. The corrugated metal of our huts was mighty thin, and the flashes showing thru the edges of our blacked out windows were not very reassuring. I don't remember any display of fear, though it was pretty obvious that we were the target of the moment.

Next morning revealed that the raiders had literally driven down our runway dropping hundreds of incendiary stick bombs and quite a number of canister type incendiary bombs. The runway was pocked, but no serious damage was done, and all was quickly patched and the runways were soon in use again. As far as I know, none of our planes or installations was hit, and no one was injured. We must have been unloaded on after failure to reach a prime target. Or—were we it?

Robert T. Sand, *P-51 ground crew, 55th Fighter Group*

With one notable exception, no one ever used our air raid shelter for its intended purpose. That would be "chicken." Instead it was used for parking bicycles and tossing beer bottles. The one exception was the night I kissed the world goodbye. At night, as was most frequent, the alert sounded and was ignored by everyone as usual. I was out with my camera and was shocked to see a buzz bomb heading straight for us from a direction 90 degrees from the usual heading. I think there was a frantic call on the Tannoy speaker to "seek shelter." In any case, it was coming fast at what seemed to be not far above tree top level.

A few hundred feet before reaching our road, the clatter of the engine suddenly stopped and the red eye stopped blinking. Knowing most of them were set to dive immediately, I hit the ground and wondered what the end would be like. After a few seconds and I was incredibly still alive, I took my hands from my ears (if it landed nearby I didn't want to lose my eardrums!) and could hear the machine whistling in a low, fast glide into a slight valley below our area, and explode. Was I scared? Yes!

But, getting back to the air raid shelter. For the first time everyone was alarmed enough to take the "seek shelter" seriously, and according to what I was told, there was a sudden invasion of the shelter (sensibly, I might add) followed by great pandemonium as bare feet found broken glass, and legs tangled with bicycle frames, resulting in our most serious injuries as a result of buzz bombs.

Arthur L. Thorsen, *P-38 pilot, 55th Fighter Group*

I don't know why I was selected for the job, but our squadron commander Major Mark Shipman picked me, I think, because he did not want to endanger the life of one of his veteran pilots. I was more expendable. The job called for aerobatics on the deck—that is ground level. Now I could do aerobatics just about as well as the next pilot, but it's much more comfortable at ten or twenty thousand feet. Rolling on the deck required ultra precision. The slightest mistake and you've "bought the farm." Combat stunting I could accept; unnecessary stunting, I felt was the domain of all the mental minus marks in the service.

I flew to a field north of London, which was a replacement depot for bomber crews who had recently arrived from training fields in the States. There existed at this station a very serious morale problem as the incoming bomber crews were made instantly aware of the high mortality rate of their brethren who had arrived earlier. Bomber Command, indeed, was suffering heavy losses. To counter this pit of despair the bomber crews found themselves in, senior officers in their infinite wisdom, decided that an air show would turn the situation around.

After landing, I taxiied behind a jeep to a designated hardstand, shut the engines down and climbed into the jeep to be driven to the Operations Shack. On the way I saw hundreds of air crew members lined up parallel to the runway I had just landed on. A flight of B-17s were preparing to take off.

At the Operations building, I reported to the officer in charge of the show, a Colonel Wilson. He introduced me to two other pilots he had been talking to. They had also been selected to take part in the impending rat race. I did not retain their names as my mind was on the challenge that lay ahead, but one, a little fellow with a moon face and a cock of the barnyard strut, was a P-51 Mustang pilot. The other officer, a P-47 Thunderbolt pilot, was a stocky, freckle-faced redhead who was rather quiet and seemed about as pleased with this assignment as I was.

Colonel Wilson said, "I'm not going to tell you boys what to do. I'm sure you can cook up something yourselves. All I ask is that you give these bomber boys something to cheer about. Show them the kind of protection they'll get when those 109s start squirting at them! Show them how you can handle those crates, but do it on the deck. You'll take off in twenty minutes. The heavies are giving them a show right now!" With that, he turned to speak to another group of officers, who were there, apparently, as spectators.

"Well," little Mustang pilot said, "I'll lead this thing." That was just about what I expected him to say.

Nelle Huse wears an officer's sheepskin jacket. She was already a widow, having lost her husband in action in the South Pacific. Nelle died shortly after attending a 55th reunion with Jan and Jack Monaghan. *Robert T. Sand*

Jan Houston brings her coffee urn in the backseat of a Jeep, and a generous portion of sunshine for the troops. *Robert T. Sand*

"Here's what we'll do. We'll take off in formation. Thunderbolt on my left, Lightning on my right." Thunderbolt pilot and I looked at each other in tacit agreement that this little runt was a fruitcake. At that moment the flight of B-17s roared down the runway at low level. When the noise subsided, Mustang pilot continued, "We'll climb to 5,000 feet, then I'll peel off, Thunderbolt second and Lightning last, all line astern. I'll pull her out on the deck and roll her right in front of the tower. You fellas' do the same."

Thunderbolt pilot and I looked at each other again. Now we were positive Mustang pilot was a fruitcake. We were all three second lieutenants so neither of us outranked the other where a question of leadership was involved. It was just that Mustang pilot was a pushy type and we were foolish enough to let him take charge. He was still babbling, "Then we'll pull up, get a little sky beneath us and do a loop, coming out of it right on the deck again, balls out! From then on, it'll be follow the leader. I'll lead. Okay?"

We both nodded to him and he lighted up a cigar that was too big for him and strolled over to a window where he could watch the heavies. Thunderbolt pilot looked at me and winked. I guess neither of us cared if Mustang pilot wanted to lead the show and have his moment of glory out front. There was still some time to kill, so Thunderbolt pilot and I sat on a bench fronting a row of lockers lining the wall at one end of the room. "You got to hand it to the little guy." he said. "He's an eager beaver. If he lives long enough, he'll be a general some day."

"He's a fruitcake," I said, and we each fired up a cigarette. At that moment a sturdy looking individual in a greasy flying suit approached, opened a locker and started getting out of his flying suit. He was a good deal older than us, probably in his early forties, stood about five ten, had a strong jaw, a thin black mustache and a day old beard. He was wearing no rank. "Hi Mac!" I greeted, "Are you flying in this stupid air show too?"

He smiled, amiably and said, "No, I just flew in to watch. Are you the fighter boys I came here to see?"

"That's right," I replied, "and it's just about time for us to get started!"

"Good luck!" he said, and Thunderbolt pilot and I walked off. Strangely, Thunderbolt pilot seemed to be walking at attention.

"Geez!" he said to me out of the corner of his mouth, "Didn't you know who that was?"

"No," I replied, nonchalantly, "He's just another pilot, isn't he?"

"Christ, no! Not *just* another pilot. That's General Bill Kepner, Commander of the whole VIII Fighter Command! He's our boss!"

I went into shock. "Good God!" I moaned, "and I called him 'Mac.' Let's get the hell out of here before he gets my name and outfit!"

"Don't worry about him," smiled Thunderbolt, "He's a great guy. He probably got a big kick outa' you."

Outside of operations, we found the little Mustang pilot waiting for us in a Jeep. "Let's use 'C' channel," he said, "In case I want to talk to you guys, okay?"

"Okay!" said I and Thunderbolt pilot in unison as we climbed into the Jeep. Shortly, we were out where our

three ships were parked on the hardstands about a quarter of a mile from the tower. The ground crews had checked them over thoroughly and topped off the gas tanks. We dropped off the Thunderbolt pilot at his ship and he winked at me again as he got out of the Jeep.

"Cheers," he said, and walked over to his ship. We pulled over to the next hardstand where the little fellow's Mustang was parked. He got out.

"Let's keep a real tight formation when we climb outa' here, then loosen it up when we go down on the deck, okay?"

"Okay!" I said, and the Jeep driver put his machine in gear and took me over to where my Lightning was crouched. The crew chief, a staff sergeant, met me. "All set?" I asked.

"Yes sir. She's a fine ship. I sure hope you fellows can buck up these air crews. Their morale isn't so hot right now."

"We'll do what we can," I said. "But to tell you the truth, Sergeant, my morale isn't so hot either." His jaw dropped and I am sure he expected a pep talk from me, but he helped me into the cockpit and into my parachute harness and shortly I was turning the engines over. I turned the radio to channel C.

Mustand pilot was already jabbering, "Got the tower okay for takeoff. Let's go boys." He pulled his Mustang out of his hardstand and taxiied in front of me, whereupon I pulled out and followed him down the taxi strip. Thunderbolt pulled out behind me. At the end of the runway, we stopped to run up our engines and check the magnetos. My engines checked out fine and apparently the others did too. We pulled out onto the runway and started our takeoff roll in formation. We were soon airborne with our wheels coming up immediately. Suddenly Mustang "fruitcake" peeled up in a tight left turn, almost driving the Thunderbolt into the ground. Thunderbolt had to slide under the Mustang and came up on my left wing. Now we were in echelon. *It's going to be a long afternoon,* I thought.

After several hundred feet of climbing, Thunderbolt slid into position on Mustang's left wing. At 5,000 feet and east of the field, the radio came to life, "Okay boys, I'm going in!" It was Mustang pilot and he peeled off and pushed into a thirty degree dive, lined up on the runway from which we had just taken off.

One of the barracks at Steeple Morden, the 355th Fighter Group base in East Anglia. The cots weren't great, but when you were always tired it didn't seem to matter. *Alexander C. Sloan via Bob Kuhnert, 355th FG Assn.*

90

A wonderful sight—the Churchill Club adjacent to Westminster Abbey in London meant some companionship and a welcome for Yanks away from home. *Mark H. Brown/USAFA*

Usually the only way to London, or any other distant destination from East Anglia, was by train. Here a train pulls into the station at Royston. *Alexander C. Sloan via Bob Kuhnert, 355th FG Assn.*

VE Day (Victory in Europe), 1945. The village of Thetford in East Anglia is festooned with Union Jacks and bustling with celebration. In the center of Eighth Air Force activity during the war, Thetford was enjoyed by crews who would pass through and stop to soak up the history and hospitality. *Mark H. Brown/USAFA*

Thunderbolt followed him by about ten ship lengths and I rolled over at an identical spacing and followed Thunderbolt.

On the way down I could see the hundreds of air crew members on the ground, watching the show. I hoped they would enjoy it. Now Mustang was levelling off on the deck and went into his roll. Suddenly a huge flame blossomed out on the runway where Mustang had been and Thunderbolt pulled out of his dive.

"Jesus Christ!" I shouted to myself, "The silly bastard let the stick come back too soon!" I had levelled off now and the Thunderbolt pulled up on my right wing. As we circled the field, I could see fire trucks, Jeeps and a meat wagon race out to where the burning and smoking wreckage lay strewn on the runway. Meat wagon hell, I thought, they'll need a vacuum cleaner to pick the little guy up.

Suddenly the radio crackled. It was Thunderbolt pilot: "I don't believe it!" he cried, "What do we do now? Fool around up here, or what?"

I punched the mike button, "Piss on it!" I shouted, "I'm going home!"

"Sounds like a good idea," he replied, "Good luck!" and he peeled off and set a heading for his home field. I did the same.

All the way back I felt sorry, more for the air crews that needed some encouragement, than I did for the Mustang pilot. What a job we did for their morale. On the other hand, looking at it realistically, we · reinforced their belief that not everyone survives this war. The experience brought back to me the words of an old RAF ditty:

A poor aviator lay dying,
At the end of a bright, summer day;
His comrades had gathered around him
To carry his pieces away.

The aircraft was stacked on his wishbone,
His machine gun was wrapped 'round his head;
A spark plug he wore on each elbow,
It was plain he'd quickly be dead.

He spit out a valve and some gaskets,
And stirred in the sump where he lay;
To mechanics who 'round him came sighing,
These are the brave words he did say.

"Take the magneto out of my stomach,
And the butterfly valve off my neck;
Tear from my liver the crankshaft,
There's a lot of good parts in this wreck.

"Take the manifold out of my left eye,
And the cylinders out of my brain;
Take the piston rods out of my kidneys,
And assemble the engine again."

Jan Houston Monaghan, *Red Cross girl, 55th Fighter Group*
In November 1944 Red Cross headquarters in London decided it was time to move Nelle [Huse] to another base where they needed a good director and to make me director at Wormingford. But when the men heard about it, they got up a petition with over 800 signatures requesting that Nelle stay at Wormingford. Headquarters gave in and I was delighted because we worked well as a team and I dreaded the thought of her leaving.

Later our teamwork prompted the commanding officer to come to us at the time he first learned the base was moving to Germany as part of the Airforce of Occupation. He asked us to accompany the base and wanted our reply before he made the official announcement to the men. Then he could say "And the Red Cross girls are coming along." We felt very honored to be recognized in that way and were happy to pack up the club and move to Kaufbeuren, Germany.

Chapter 5

Ground Crews

Robert T. Sand, *propeller shop, 55th Fighter Group*

The men who worked on the line consisted of everything from saints to knaves. They did share one thing in common: total dedication to their jobs and to the safety of the men who flew their airplanes. This means everyone from the line chief, who was a master sergeant, down to the privates. The mechanics were concerned that the engines could survive a 900 mile trip

The ground crew for Lt. William "Hank" Gruber services *Cooter* at Leiston, England, home of the 357th Fighter Group. *J. E. Frary*

Crew Chief T/Sgt. Roger Fraleigh and Sgt. Bob Sand on the line at Wormingford, home of the 55th Fighter Group. *Robert T. Sand*

at peak performance. The radio men knew that communication during the long flights, and during combat, was a matter of life or death. Armorers, too, were very conscious of the fact that all machine guns must work smoothly, bomb racks must release belly tanks or bombs when commanded, or the plane would be greatly handicapped in combat. During those years up to the end of the war, I never knew a man who didn't do his best.

Whenever there was any kind of crash, or a plane failed to return from a mission, the crew of that plane was in a state of great apprehension until proven that no maintenance fault was the cause. The propeller department was even more concerned because it worked on every plane in the squadron. Not only the fighter planes, but the training planes and the officers' own "air taxis."

When we could, we watched every plane take off, and when possible watched them land. This was particularly so when combat missions were involved. At the end of a mission we anxiously awaited the reports from the crew chiefs all down the line, hoping for a clear report.

We still remember the anxiety we felt regarding the [P-38's] Curtiss-Electric constant speed propeller. It was a clever design but prone to troubles. On some planes the carbon brushes that carried the circuits from the static engine to the rotating propeller wore out excessively fast or sometimes snapped off. Sometimes electrical relays failed, or points would carbon up, or fuse together. An

The right engine on this 55th Fighter Group P-38 has just stopped turning at Wormingford. During a massive dogfight with German fighters, the Lightning had a mid-air collision with another of the unit's fighters, which did not come home. The left engine is feathered and the ground crew are clearly astonished at what they see. *Robert T. Sand*

96

Nuthampstead, 27 December 1943. T/Sgt. Roger Fraleigh spots his P–38, flown by Lt. Ernest Marcy, as fellow ground crew member Nick Lippucci looks on. *Robert T. Sand*

Bonds between ground crew and pilot became very strong in spite of the distinct divisions the Army made between enlisted men and officers. Crew Chief Sgt. Don Allen and pilot Lt. Marvin Arthur, 4th Fighter Group, stand in front of their *Davey Lee,* named after Arthur's son. Allen had crewed the Mustang during Clarence Boretsky's entire tour, when it was named *Meg,* then repainted the nose art for Arthur and stayed on as crew chief. Ground crews came to have an uncanny ability for keeping their aircraft in top shape. *Donald E. Allen*

When major inspections were due, the maintenance hangar crew became involved in the process with the regular ground crew. The Mustangs of the 4th Fighter Group, as with most Eighth Air Force units, were exceptionally well cared for. Here Don Allen shares a moment with hangar crew mechanic Chuck Bowen. Don is wearing the highly prized sheepskin jacket which fighter pilots found impossible to wear in the confines of the P–51's cockpit. *Donald E. Allen*

97

improper connection could cause one propeller to increase pitch and the other to decrease pitch. Even worse it was possible that one prop could feather up entirely—or if an engine failed and needed the prop feathered but failed to work, could cause that prop to windmill causing a great drag on that side of the airplane, with disastrous results.

The fact that we had Harold Melby, one of the best prop men in the Army Air Force, to head up our department accounts for the fact that as far as we know, our planes had no accidents due to prop failure. He would frequently have us review every wiring connection, every adjustment to bell-crank control, all governor and relay tolerances over and over so they

would be indelibly fixed in our minds. Then he would test us, and boy! We'd better get it right! We didn't resent this discipline as we were well aware of what a critical difference it could make.

Eventually we could pat ourselves on the back because both the Curtiss-Electric and the Hamilton Standard propeller reps who called on

Don Allen (right) and his best buddy in the service, Jerry Byrge, served as crew for *Blondie,* Marvin Arthur's new Mustang that replaced *Davey Lee.* Allen's talent for nose art is more than evident here. He was responsible for most of the outstanding nose art in the 4th Fighter Group's 334th Fighter Squadron. *Donald E. Allen*

us from time to time told us we were the best prop crew in the UK, and that they didn't call on us to teach us anything, but to learn from us. *That* was our best medal! Of course, they may have told that to *all* the girls. We took it at face value, though.

Kermit Riem, our second in charge, was also a meticulous and sharp trouble-shooter. He could easily have headed up his own department, but as it was he made an ideal fellow crew member. Aside from that, he helped our morale with his cheerful nature and sense of humor. Why shouldn't he? He had a great gal back home whom he married before going overseas. Harold found his bride in England and was married there. Both couples are still dancing up a storm every week!

Arthur L. Thorsen, *P-38 pilot, 55th Fighter Group*

When I got out on the line, I found Sergeant Harmon tracing down a hydraulic leak that my aircraft had

Lt. Col. Everett W. Stewart helps a passenger strap into the 4th Fighter Group's first two-seater Mustang at Debden. This war-weary P–51B, converted by T/Sgt. Woody Jensen, carried all three squadron colors on the rudder and WD–2 on the side. It was a huge success with ground crew, not to mention girlfriends smuggled in by pilots who wanted to make the ultimate impression. *Edward B. Richie*

developed. While he was busy at that task, I put in a little more cockpit time to refresh my memory on the location of all switches and instruments. It might seem strange that after more than 230 hours in the aircraft, I would still have to familiarize myself with what made it go [but] when you're spending hours, weaving over the bombers, you can't pass the time examining your cockpit setup. I was a slow study to begin with and felt pretty lucky I knew where all the instruments were and how to use them.

Every time I caught Sergeant Harmon's eye, he seemed to be grinning. Once he said, "Found a shell hole in your right, rear boom the other day, Lieutenant. It's patched up now." I crawled out of the airplane and went back to inspect the repair job, feeling a slight flutter under my breast bone. "Want me to fix you up with another rear view mirror?" he asked.

"What's that supposed to mean?" I grinned, sheepishly.

"Just that someone must have snuck up on you while you had your head up your can."

I appreciated the high level of respect that my fatherly crew chief had for young officers and after receiving a brief lecture on how to care for "his" airplane, I was allowed to pedal my bicycle back to the barracks area.

Robert T. Sand, *P-51 ground crew, 55th Fighter Group*

Have rather enjoyed the change in jobs since being put on a [P-51] crew. The hours of work are slightly longer, but I can see where the prop man has the most work, which is a revelation to me, after all of the ribbing we have always taken. I can see now that the ribbing was a defensive mechanism. And as to deserving ratings, I am more sure than ever that myself and Stivason were

Debden sported one of the most colorful Mustangs flying when the 335th Squadron's converted, war-weary two-seater P-51B was painted the same overall red carried on the group's aircraft noses. Though it was technically an OTU (operational training unit) aircraft used for pilot familiarization, it saw more use giving rides to ground crews who deserved a taste of what they had worked so hard to keep flying. *Edward B. Richie*

treated unjustly by denying us our authorized ratings of staff sergeant and buck sergeant respectively when we had P-38s.

The ratings were given to other departments in which they were not authorized. Now, however, with single engine ships, we have more ratings than would ordinarily be allowed, so chances are even less of getting anywhere. It isn't the money so much, but the fact that I still pull all the details of a raw recruit while all of my old buddies have long ago graduated from that realm.

Jack Monaghan, *maintenance supply, 55th Fighter Group*

Just before D-day everybody on the base was a painter—officers, enlisted men. Everybody from top to bottom was out on the line painting black and white stripes on the wings and bodies of all the planes so they could be identified by our troops as they were landing on D-day. In the process everything was shut down. Nobody could get on or off the base.

Unfortunately there were some girls from neighboring farms who had

Damn great Merlin out front . . . that's how most Mustang pilots felt about the Packard-built Rolls-Royce engine that pulled them into combat. Lt. Robert E. Woody's 355th Fighter Group P–51B, *Woody's Maytag,* swallows up crew chief Bill Gertzen during some routine maintenance at Steeple Morden. *Alexander C. Sloan via Bob Kuhnert, 355th FG Assn.*

lost cows on the base. They—and their cows—were put in quarantine and could not go home. The next thing we knew there were a bunch of farmers storming onto the base to see the commanding officer, demanding their daughters be allowed to go home. They were quickly put in quarantine also. They finally quieted down enough to listen to what was happening. The day they had been waiting for all the years was finally here. When they registered what was going on, they stayed put.

It so happened that same night a heavy fog rolled in and our group found they were painting not only our own planes but those of two or three British squadrons that had found their

own bases closed in the fog and ours was the only place they could land. I don't know how long or how many planes we painted but we had our own outfit—the 38th, 338th and 343rd—plus two or three squadrons of British bombers and some night fighters. Everybody was tired but glad the invasion was at last starting.

Every now and then as we painted, we would stop because we could hear the buzz bombs chugging straight down the middle of the runways and we waited to see what would happen. Buzz bomb engines might cut out and they might go a mile or two or they might stop dead and come straight in. We never knew. Everyone would stop painting while

the buzz bomb chugged over our field and went on. We never did know where some of them hit.

Robert T. Sand, *propeller shop 55th Fighter Group*

When P-38s were pioneering the long distance fighter sweeps, of course the kidneys didn't stop working on these many hours long flights, so Lockheed included a urinal dubbed a relief tube. This consisted of a stiff, cylindrical tube of black rubber, designed to fit the average pilot. From this a smaller flexible tube led to the underside trailing edge of the wing. There it exited into a little fairing with an opening of a couple of square inches facing away from the

Dawn seeps through the fog and into a 55th Fighter Group maintenance hangar at Wormingford, 19 May 1944. P-38s that have required major work during the night will be pulled out on the line by the Cletrac tug near the door. This amazing little tracked vehicle could pull just about anything through mud, snow and slime. *Robert T. Sand*

slipstream, hence causing a vacuum to evacuate the tube. Evidently the designer had not flight tested it.

After one of these grueling missions, a very tired pilot dragged himself out of the plane, saying to his crew chief, "Causey, can't you do something about this relief tube? I had to take a leak and it came back and soaked my pants and made a helluva mess!"

The pilot stalked wearily to the jeep, leaving the crew chief scratching his head. After giving it a good think, he went to the engineering shack, got a piece of sheet aluminum, some snips, a drill and some rivets. He then fashioned a sort of reverse scoop like half of a funnel, and attached it in place of the former tiny one. The new one was like four or five inches across at the large end facing to the rear.

"This should solve the problem," he mused, then forgot all about it.

When the pilot returned from the next mission, the crew chief raised the canopy and started releasing the pilot's harness, to be greeted with, "Causey, what in hell did you do to that relief tube? When I had to take a leak I got the damn thing within 6 inches of my peter, and Whap!, it popped right in, and when I finished I thought I'd *never* get it out again!"

So, we all made special trips to see this engineering marvel. We noted, though, that no other pilots requested this modification. The poor crew chief never did get a medal for innovation.

Arthur L. Thorsen, *P-38 pilot, 55th Fighter Group*

I landed at Wormingford and taxied to my hardstand where Sergeant Harmon and the rest of my crew waited for me. The ground crews are very special people. They watch you take off for a mission, then wait in the dispersal area for your return, greeting you with broad smiles of relief. All of the pilots are touched by this display of faithfulness and affection, and though few of them will comment on it, the warm feeling between pilot and crew is there, nevertheless.

When I shut down my engines and cut the switches, I began to tremble, first mildly, then growing in intensity. I was bathed in sweat and soon realized I was too weak to crawl out of the cockpit. Sergeant Harmon and Sergeant Shieny had to help me out of the cockpit, then off the wing of the aircraft and onto the waiting truck that would take me back to the 38th Squadron pilot's room. As the truck pulled away, Sergeant Hadsel, my armorer, noticing that the tape had been blown away from the muzzles of my guns, gave me a thumbs up sign. The ground crews delight in their

This is what close formation practice resulted in at times. M/Sgt. "Heine" Ziegler, A flight line chief, and crew chief T/Sgt. Richard Bock change the damaged rudder, Bob Sand helped replace the pro- peller on the other ship. Both Mustangs were lucky to make it back. *Robert T. Sand*

pilot's claims, because it's their ship and they're just as proud as if they squeezed the triggers themselves.

As the truck rumbled along, I wondered about my seizure of trembling. It must be some kind of delayed action. It was fear, of course, and that was the strange part of it all. It occurred to me that, while in the air and even in combat, I was not afraid, but as soon as I was safe on the ground, fear set in. I wondered if the others in the truck felt the same way now, but I didn't ask.

Jan Houston Monaghan, *Red Cross girl, 55th Fighter Group*

Every morning we took turns driving our little Hillman car around the line with coffee for the men who were "sweating out" the planes. Sometimes we had to pull off on the side as the planes taxied by before takeoff but usually they were long gone and the Red Cross coffee van provided a welcome break in the dreary waiting period. The hardest time for the men was when the planes were coming home and theirs was not among them. Ground crews became very possessive of their planes and pilots and never forgot them. Pilots, in return, never forgot their lives

The 56th Fighter Group Thunderbolts on the line at Boxted in late summer, 1944. Drop tanks have been spread around for use at the numerous hardstands and the aircraft are slowly coming back up to operational status for the next mission. *Mark H. Brown/USAFA*

104

depended on the careful maintenance of their planes by their crews.

When the winter winds whistled across the airfield, Nelle and I found our slacks and jackets weren't very warm. Feeling sorry for the shivering Red Cross girls, the men at Air Corps Supply issued us leather fleece-lined flying suits and boots that were no longer being worn by the pilots since P-51s replaced the P-38s. We resembled funny brown bears as we plodded around but were we warm!

Our coffee van was always received with smiles and the question, "How's the coffee?" and sometimes I would have to admit, "It tastes like the shavings from the pencil sharpener but you can warm your hands on the cup."

Robert T. Sand, *P-51 ground crew, 55th Fighter Group*

Ground personnel were gleeful targets for playful pilots, and more than once I hit the sod or dove off my bike as a P-51 streaked down the perimeter track at close to 400 mph with prop tips only about a foot above the asphalt. I remember once as we got up and were dusting ourselves off, someone said, "Good God, did you notice we were looking down on *top* of his wing!" Another time I was on my bike in an exposed area on the perimeter when I saw this guy coming in a long power dive. I thought it was for scaring hell out of me, but he apparently didn't have that in mind as he passed at a respectable distance. Strange, but those buzz jobs remain among my fondest memories of those days. It was pure envy!

Jack Monaghan, *maintenance supply, 55th Fighter Group*

Two fellows called Younger and Rampke were old buddies from way

A 62nd Squadron, 56th Fighter Group P-47D is getting a thorough going over before its next mission over enemy territory. All eight machine guns have been removed for servicing and ammo sits ready to be loaded from the wooden boxes in front of each wing and the fuel truck is running. Soon the drop tanks will be hung and the fighter will be ready. *Mark H. Brown/USAFA*

With drop-tank crates spread across the field at Honington, 364th Fighter Group ground crew bring their P–51Ds back to operational status. The enlisted men who kept the Eighth Air Force's fighters airworthy rarely got a full-night's sleep. Up long before the pilots, they would make sure their assigned aircraft were loaded and run-up. After group takeoff they supposedly had some time to sleep, but nervous worry about their pilots and aircraft would make them "sweat out" the mission and pace the field until the first sight of returning fighters. After the mission the aircraft required extensive attention, often late into the night when the entire cycle started again. *Mark H. Brown/USAFA*

back. They had gone into the service together and always went to town together. One night they were out on the town and when they returned to the base, Rampke was stopped by the MPs. He gave them some lip and was promptly arrested and thrown in the brig.

As it so happened, Younger was slow getting out of the truck and Rampke was gone by the time he got there. When he learned what had happened to Rampke, Younger promptly went to the squadron area and got on the phone. He called the MPs. A Captain was on duty that night, and he said to them, "You have a man there by the name of Sergeant Rampke. I want him out of the Brig now. This is Colonel Younger on the base and I want him released immediately."

The MPs had no idea who Colonel Younger was, they'd never heard of him but they released Rampke anyhow because a colonel had told them to.

From that day on T/Sgt. Ralph Younger was called The Colonel.

Robert E. Kuhnert, *radio line chief, 355th Fighter Group*

As radio maintenance line chief, it was my responsibility to see that the communications equipment (VHF radio, SCR–522) was operable in all

Crew chief S/Sgt. Don Allen sits on the wing of Lt. Clarence L. Boretsky's 4th Fighter Group P–51D *Meg.* Metal drop tanks have been placed on the ground, ready for installation. As Allen recalled, "There were a few sandbag revetments for parking the 'kites' at Debden but most sat out in the open, some on concrete pads, others on the interlocked metal sheeting. Metal drop tanks were usually ready to go, complete with two little glass elbows on each to provide the 'breakaway' when released from the bomb rack." *Donald E. Allen*

squadron airplanes. Our technicians worked long hours, cold nights to keep the equipment operable.

Major Claiborne H. Kinnard came to us as 354th Fighter Squadron CO in late 1943 (from the 356th FG). He had problems with his ears, as later confirmed by our squadron flight surgeon, Dr. R. A. Fontenot. Kinnard was grounded for a short time because of it.

On many missions Major Kinnard returned complaining that he could not hear. My communications officer, Lt. Stan Clark, twisted the field phone immediately after mission de-briefing to ask what was wrong with Major Kinnard's airplane. A check-out immediately after the plane landed usually revealed a perfectly working radio. My reply to my boss was, "Nothing wrong, sir; his radio works fine."

After several such complaints, followed by the same response from me—which was not being accepted by Major Kinnard, nor by a frustrated Lieutenant Clark—I was finally given a stern order: "Find something wrong with it and fix it!"

Needless to say, there was much activity in an attempt to find something wrong and fix it. We tried many different receivers, resulting in no apparent difference. We checked wiring harness bundles, changed dynamotors (radio power supply), strung a new co-ax cable from radio set to antenna. We even added a

Capt. Jerry H. Ayers, 55th Fighter Group, has just landed at Nuthampstead in the early evening of 29 November 1943 after getting his first kill. Crew Chief T/Sgt. Ralph Sexton (left) and assistant Sgt. "Irish" O'Flaherty are intent on hearing the full story upon climbing up onto the P-38 after shutdown. *Robert T. Sand*

108

The Mary N II gets washed down, scrubbed and scoured by its crew chief at Debden. Whatever it took, the ground crews did, not only to keep the aircraft running, but to keep them looking like polished race cars. Note the oil trail from the engine breather tube on the side of the cowling. This usually spread back across the fuselage, but the crewman has already cleaned it off to just short of the leading edge, most likely with high-octane fuel. Red tape has been placed over the .50 caliber machine gun muzzles after reloading. *Edward B. Richie*

second antenna (the IFF antenna) to the receiver, in case he was experiencing blocking by wing or tail.

Nothing changed; the radio worked fine but pilot Kinnard could not hear away from base. To satisfy the order handed down we turned to our "4th Echelon Shop," which performed heavy, internal maintenance on equipment which could not be done on the line. S/Sgt Warren Brainard and his workmates devised a solution. They added a separate tube, another stage of amplification, to a receiver, increasing audio power output to rival the "boom boxes" today's youth carry around.

Eureka! Problem solved! Major Kinnard can hear. We kept that one specially-modified receiver for him alone. When it needed maintenance it was removed from the airplane, checked, and returned to his airplane only. All other airplanes were maintained by a "black box" swap procedure from the supply of repaired radios on our shop shelf.

In my frustration to find a solution I mentally hatched a fiendish method which I threatened to employ.

Ground crew mix with pilots of the 55th Fighter Group after the unit's return from what turned out to be the Eighth Air Force's biggest mission of World War II, 24 December 1944. From left to right: M/Sgt. Robert Tudor (line chief), S/Sgt. Nick Lippucci, S/Sgt. Fred Rumley, T/Sgt. Roger Fraleigh (crew chief of CG-R behind), Cpl. Herb Heichelbech, Sgt. "Frog" Sheen, Lt. Bob Maloney, Maj. John D. Landers (38th Squadron CO) and S/Sgt. Francis O'Leary. Landers is clearly happy about the 38th scoring four of the Group's fifteen confirmed kills that day. *Robert T. Sand*

(I voiced the threat in very close circles, well away from the CO, else I might still be breaking rocks at Leavenworth.) My ingenious procedure would have been to connect a wire to the 300 volt output of the dynamotor, string it unnoticed into the cockpit, under the pilot's seat, and connect it to a fine wire circle in the pilot's relief tube. My medical hypothesis was that if he used the relief tube at altitude the resultant jolt would surely clear his ears. (I have had no confirmation of this procedure from the medical community.)

Happily for all concerned— especially a certain technical sergeant—the highly advanced experimental procedure was not needed: the problem was solved through a more orthodox and acceptable approach.

Jan Houston Monaghan, *Red Cross girl, 55th Fighter Group*

Since only the pilots flew on a fighter base, there were a lot of boring hours for the ground crews. We tried at the Red Cross Club to find different types of programs: concerts, lectures, dances, snooker and ping-pong tournaments to satisfy the varied interests of the men. Birthday parties each month for those with birthdays had the traditional ice cream and cake. Sometimes when we heard that an officer had a birthday, we would invite him to our Red Cross office for "afternoon tea" with special sandwiches and cake.

One day I said to Nelle [Huse], "Tomorrow is Colonel [Elwyn] Righetti's birthday. Let's invite him for a really nice tea."

"We have too much to do this week, Jan, we don't have time for that tomorrow," said Nelle. "We'll do something special for him next week."

I always wondered afterwards . . . if we'd invited him, would he have come? And if he had come, he wouldn't have flown that day. But he flew . . . on his birthday . . . and was shot down.

Arthur O. Beimdiek, *P-38 pilot, 14th Fighter Group*

I had much compassion for my crew chief and the others too. Stop and think about it. If their plane did not make it home, they never knew, for sure, whether it was their fault or the enemy's. After one raid, I was so full of holes I stopped at a base called Ferriana which was south of Constantine [in northern Algeria]. The rest of the flight went on home. When I didn't peel off with the others, they told me my crew chief sat on an ammunition box and cried like a baby. The others in the flight told him I sat down for emergency patching and would be along later. When I got back, he was waiting for me with a bottle he had been saving.

Jan Houston Monaghan, *Red Cross girl, 55th Fighter Group*

When the Red Cross snack bar was especially busy, we knew the mess that night must have been inedible. We spent many hours in the evening visiting with fellows in the snack bar, listening to their gripes, sharing their homesickness, admiring pictures of their girlfriends, wives, children, and rejoicing with them when they had good news from home.

Sometimes on dance nights or after weekend passes, fellows would show up three sheets to the wind from a few too many drinks. We quickly learned to laugh with the funny ones as we moved them to the door, to manipulate the argumentative ones and to maneuver with gentle persuasion the mean drunks. We rarely had a problem but if we did, we had plenty of willing helpers standing by.

Chapter 6

Nose Art

Robert T. Sand, *propeller shop, 55th Fighter Group*

During those first weeks at Nuthampstead I did a few "nose art" jobs for some of the pilots. One was for Captain Joe Myers. He took me to his plane and described what he wanted.

"I want a skull, as gruesome as you can make it. Have blood dripping all over it, and, under the skull, written in blood, put 'Journey's End.'"

Propeller shop Sergeant Bob Sand did some five nose art paintings for 55th Fighter Group P–38s, including *Texas Ranger* for group CO Col. Jack S. Jenkins. Another pilot bellied the original plane in and the armament door was transferred to Jenkins' new Lightning, as is evident here due to the missing section of painted-on rope. "My main memory," recalls Sand, "is of working on this all night a couple of nights and of my boss' displeasure at my not showing up for work til 9 a.m." *Robert T. Sand*

Capt. Joseph Myers' *Journey's End* of the 38th Squadron, 55th Fighter Group, painted by Sgt. Bob Sand. The crew stands in front of the Lightning, 18 November 1943; left to right: Nick Lippucci, armorer K. P. Bartozeck, crew chief J. D. "Dee Dee" Durnin, assistant crew chief Fred Rumley (known as a most persuasive philosopher on *any* subject). *Robert T. Sand*

I was appalled, but I was also awed by the fact that he was one of the most admired and daring of our pilots, and also by those bright and shiny captain's bars.

I stammered that I thought the idea was much too gory.

"Well, you can leave off the blood on the skull, but will you write 'Journey's End' in blood?"

The talent was doubtful, and I didn't have the proper colors for the job, but, of course, I said I would try.

One day, from across the dispersal area, I looked up to see a P-38 wallowing in a stall only about fifty feet off the ground. It dropped from my sight and a big cloud of what

I first thought to be smoke, but turned out to be dust, appeared.

Later, when I was free to go to the scene, I entered the area with my camera. It was chaos. The '38 had come down, colliding with a fuel tanker truck, turning it over on its back, bounced into at least one parked P-38, perhaps two, and came to rest upside down, partly on one of the P-38s. 150 octane gasoline had poured in a fast-spreading lake over the entire area. The pilot was hanging by his harness, stunned and unable to free himself. Men from the line ran in across the gasoline-soaked ground. One shut off switches and disconnected the battery, as some

motors were still sparking. At least two men opened the canopy, and, taking the weight of the pilot on their shoulders, unsnapped the harness and eased him to the ground. Observing first aid procedures as well as possible, but expecting the gasoline to go up any second, they dragged or carried him beyond the danger area and laid him on a blanket.

According to angry crew members who had been on the scene, and who told me this part of the story, the rescuers were not commended for their deed, but actually "chewed out" by the doctor for moving an injured man. This in spite of the fact that they, and all of us, had taken first aid

Skylark IV was painted on Maj. Mark W. Shipman's Lightning by Bob Sand. Yet to be added was one Italian fascist symbol from a kill during Shipman's tour with the 48th Fighter Squadron in North Africa.

Standing to the left is armorer Sergeant Westman, with crew chief T/Sgt. "Fox" Nelson, 18 November 1943. *Robert T. Sand*

Capt. Jerry H. Ayers stands with his crew in front of *Mountain Ayers,* one of Bob Sand's favorite creations. "This was a labor of love, partly because I, like everyone else, had great respect and admiration for Capt. Ayers. He was a real, and unassuming, gentleman. He was so appreciative, which was not usually the case with others. These quite crude efforts were done on very cold nights, with runny paints, usually not being completed until four or five a.m., and a full work day before and after at the regular job, and without pay, out of respect for the men who were putting their lives on the line. So, a 'thank you' was like a pat on the head to a puppy. It made one glow! The enlisted men were saddened by Capt. Ayers' ear problems, which restricted his flying career. In our estimation he was an extremely talented pilot. The old mountaineer, by the way, outlasted all the other insignias. We figured that he had at least 150 missions over enemy territory, some sort of record." *Robert T. Sand*

114

Nooky Booky IV was flown by 357th Fighter Group ace Leonard K. "Kit" Carson. Unable to get into Leiston due to poor weather, several of the unit's P-51s landed at Wormingford on Christmas Day 1944 after escorting bombers over Germany. *Robert T. Sand*

Originally the mount of 357th Fighter Group pilot Arval J. Roberson, *Passion Wagon* was passed on to Charles E. Weaver, then given to yet another pilot. The early morning frost, 26 December 1944, has retained the chill of the cold Christmas holiday missions flown by the Eighth Air Force. Ground crew would shortly be trying to get the Mustangs ready to head back to Leiston from Wormingford. Bob Sand had to help: "My memory is of washing down iced wings and tail surfaces with rags and gallons of ethylene glycol, and frozen bare hands." *Robert T. Sand*

courses, and knew the risk. There just was no choice. They deserved a medal.

The pilot had a sore neck and back for a while, then returned to flying duty. He expressed his gratitude to his rescuers, whose names I once knew, but have forgotten. It would be nice to find that this young man had survived the war, was still alive, and could tell us this story himself.

So, coming upon the crash scene just described, what do I see in the middle of all this carnage, and the cause of all this mess, but Joe Myers' plane, *Journey's End*. Here was this badly damaged plane upside down and partially supported by another P-38. Its twin tails pointed crazily to the sky—and plainly, upside down, on its nose, the perfect title for this scene, "Journey's End."

It made such a fantastic subject that I lined it up in the viewfinder of my little Kodak Pony and prepared to snap the picture of a lifetime. Then an alarm buzzer went off in my head. "Whoa! You may get into trouble here. There may be a security violation you don't even know about."

So, regretfully, I lowered the camera and the scene went un-recorded.

James R. Hanson, *P-51 pilot, 339th Fighter Group*

As we fly on towards France I find myself humming the music from Ravel's "Bolero" to the steady throb of my beautiful Rolls-Royce engine. The music seems to fit right in with the smooth throb of the engine which is like drums in the background. The ever increasing tempo and volume of the music matches my increasing tension as we approach the enemy coast. The music builds and gets faster until finally it seems to spin wildly and crash into silence. Just as we've crossed inland several bursts of flak break the spell and I'm back to reality. I have the name for my plane now, *Bolero*.

Robert T. Sand, *Propeller shop, 55th Fighter Group*

One time I had the ignominy of watching a P-38 belly in which had one of my nose art jobs painted on its armament door. This was *Texas Ranger* made for Col. Jack S. Jenkins. Colonel Jenkins allowed a friend to borrow the plane, and he bellied it in at another field. The armament door was retrieved and installed on Colonel Jenkins' new P-38 with the missing parts of the lariat smudged in hastily by someone else. This plane came to a bad end too, and may have been the one I saw belly in. It seems there was a third plane this happened to. I found that armament door in a stack of

Charles W. Reed flew *Princess Pat* with the 63rd Fighter Squadron, 56th Fighter Group. In the background another group P-47 still carries the white nose marking which adorned all Eighth AF fighters until various colors were chosen to differentiate groups from each other. *Alexander C. Sloan via Bob Kuhnert, 355th FG Assn.*

When Lt. Marvin Arthur had crew chief S/Sgt. Don Allen paint the nose art on his new aircraft, he wanted it named after his wife, Blondie. Here Don admires his vision of loveliness and, as he recalls, *Blondie* "was the name of his wife, but the painting was strictly from my imagination—sexy, but covered. It appears I got a new sheepskin jacket to go with the new plane. It seemed we only discarded this garb for about six weeks in mid-summer. It felt good to be warm when the pesky wind was always blowing." *Donald E. Allen*

117

scrap aluminum, undamaged, but disgraced. I'm sure it was bad for Colonel Jenkins' morale, and it didn't do mine any good either.

Much later, when P-38s were being retired and replaced by P-51s, I felt exonerated when a P-38 carrying my whimsy of nose art *Mountain Ayers* was cited for having made at least 150 missions over enemy territory, which was considered to be a sort of record, at least in our outfit.

This was made for Capt. Jerry H. Ayers. When he left the plane, others flew with his logo.

Well, at least the good and the bad neutralized each other!

Capt. Jim Duffy greets the 354th Fighter Squadron mascot bulldog "Yank" shortly after landing at Steeple Morden in his *Dragon Wagon.* According to Bob Kuhnert, the well-bred English canine, whose sire was owned by Winston Churchill, was bought at a dog show in Duxford by Buck Wrightam, Harold Berg and I. C. Myers. Buck decreed he would be the squadron mascot, suggesting all personnel be called "The Bulldogs." Squadron CO Claiborne Kinnard liked the idea, put the existing unit bulldog logo in a circle and placed "The Bulldogs" across the Statue of Liberty in the background, thus creating the definitive 354th Squadron patch issued to the troops. "Bulldogs" was painted above the exhaust stacks on many of the unit's P-51s. After the war Myers brought Yank home in his duffle bag. Yank was sedated before the trip to avoid alerting inspectors. They made it safely to Camp Shanks, then home to Seymour, Missouri. *USAF/NASM*

118

Ted Lines' first *Thunder Bird,* a P–51B, gets the nose art treatment. The motif was natural for the 4th Fighter Group pilot because he came from Mesa, Arizona, with its rich American Indian heritage. *Edward B. Richie*

119

Though this nose art did not belong to his P-38, Lt. Alvan DeForge is clearly delighted to stand next to it on the 82nd Fighter Group line at Foggia, Italy. *Walter E. Zurney*

120

The nose art on Lt. Albert P. Knafelz' 62nd Fighter Squadron, 56th Fighter Group P-47D was fanciful and poignant at the same time— *Staglag Luft III . . . I Wanted Wings. Mark H. Brown/USAFA*

Lt. Arthur R. Bowers in the cockpit of his P-51D *Sweet Arlene*. Don Allen painted the nose art from a snapshot of Bowers' wife. *Donald E. Allen*

Col. Dave Schilling, commander of the 56th Fighter Group, taxies out for a mission in his camouflaged P-47D, which bears the "Li'l Abner" comic strip character "Hairless Joe." The 56th had several Thunderbolts adorned with Al Capp's creations, each done in impeccably faithful style to the originals. *Mark H. Brown/USAFA*

Leland P. "Tommy" Molland's 308th Fighter Squadron Spitfire Mk. VIII *Fargo Express* in Italy, January 1944. The single white swastika denotes a confirmed kill while the black swastikas stood for probables.

By the time Molland ended his tour, he had a total of 11 confirmed kills—four in Spitfires, seven in Mustangs. *William J. Skinner*

Capt. Dick Perley, 313th Fighter Squadron, with his P-47D *Kandy K II* at Toul-Ochey airfield, near Nancy, France in the spring of 1945. The squadron nose artist, Sgt. Lester L. Schaufler, was one of those extremely talented men who painted numerous aircraft throughout the war, including Perley's Thunderbolts. *Richard H. Perley*

Chapter 7

Long Range Escort

William E. Kepner, *Commander, VIII Fighter Command*

About the first of August, 1943, two experiments began, one necessitated by the other, which, by some vision and much trial and error, were to make possible the first really long range fighter escort. These were the use of belly tanks or wing tanks and the group by group relay system.

Putting belly tanks on the Thunderbolts for longer range seems simple enough but the program was complicated by tactical considerations. Since our fighters were liable to attack or be attacked the minute they crossed the enemy coast, there was hope only of saving the distance out across the Channel, and a tank of but 75 gallons capacity was used for this purpose. The hopes of high Air Force Command were of course looking far beyond the modest achievement and these hopes received new impetus one day when the 4th Group took a chance and carried their tanks inland, holding them to the moment of

124

combat. 56th and other Groups followed suit.

With this possibility demonstrated, larger and larger tanks were requested and became available. Farther and farther went the Thunderbolts along with the Fortresses and Liberators, escorting them 450 miles now to any point within an arc range running approximately through Kiel, Hanover, Karlsruhe, Stuttgart, Vichy, Limoges, LaRochelle. The enemy tried early attacks upon our fighters to force them to drop tanks. It was too costly for him. He relapsed into his policy of avoiding fighter combat whenever possible in order to get at bombers when, in the last reaches of their penetration, they were still unescorted. His opportunity to do this was now cut down to a very much shorter period on the deepest missions and on the middle distance missions did not exist at all. Long-range escort was actually in being.

Since the faster speed of our fighters caused them to use up their

range in a much shorter period of time than bombers covering the same distance, it became necessary to divide up our fighter escort into relays. A group would fly direct to a rendezvous point along the bomber route, stay with the bombers until relieved by another group or as long as possible, then return more or less directly to base. The long line of bombers was protected not only by the fighter groups assigned for its protection for certain divisions for given periods but also by the constant stream of fighters en route to rendezvous or returning from escort pretty much along the same route. Experience taught many lessons and this relay system became a large and permanent feature in the new aerial warfare science of long-range escort.

The addition to our fighter force operations in October and December 1943 groups of P-38 Lightnings created a new phase. With new built-in fuel capacity adding to their normal long range, the P-38s could go to the bombers' target and provide

Dawn, 11 December 1944, 55th Fighter Group, Wormingford. The Eighth Air Force launches its largest raid of the war so far with all bomb and fighter groups participating; 1,586 bombers and 841 fighters were dispatched. "By 0300 hours," said Bob Sand, "the air was one great drone of engines as bombers slowly formed enormous formations from horizon to horizon. Our Mustangs, being faster, were scheduled to leave some three hours after the bombers . . . crews are gathering around the aircraft, waiting for that moment. What a paradox. These scenes show death en masse, yet it was one of the most incredibly beautiful scenes I have ever witnessed." Assistant crew chief Alabama Norris, Lieutenant Cox and Capt. Bob Maloney gather on the wing of Sand's P-51 to watch the spectacle. *Robert T. Sand*

125

protection there during the most crucial moments of bombing. Still, there were gaps in the escort. There were not enough P-38s to cover the bombers from the point where the Thunderbolts had finally to leave them and return and still cover the target area too. . . .

Complete long-range fighter escort, round trip from England to Berlin, Munich and points east became possible with the addition to the operations of [VIII Fighter] Command in March 1944 of a number of groups of P-51 Mustangs, by large measure longer in range than any other fighter on the battle fronts and superior in many other combat characteristics. The circle was now complete. . . .

If it can be said that the P-38s struck the Luftwaffe in its vitals and the P-51s [gave] the coup de grace, it was the Thunderbolt that broke its back.

James H. Doolittle, *Commander, Eighth Air Force*

Adolf Galland said that the day we took our fighters off the bombers and put them against the German fighters—that is, went from defensive to offensive—Germany lost the air war. . . . I made that decision and it was my most important decision during World War II. As you can imagine, the bomber crews were upset. The fighter pilots were ecstatic.

David C. Schilling, *P-47 pilot, 56th Fighter Group*

On several occasions the rumor has been spread that we left the bombers entirely and went down to 10,000 feet or below and engaged enemy aircraft and came home. We have, but because there were large numbers beneath the bombers, climbing and waiting for us to leave. At the time the bombers were not under attack and our fuel was getting very low. If we could disperse and destroy them before we were forced to

The Eighth Air Force used metal and paper drop tanks, both of which can be seen here. The paper tanks appear brighter because they are painted with silver dope. Due to the desire to save strategic metals, the British came up with a system of making laminated and glued paper that would hold fuel—for just one mission. If fuel was left in the tanks for more than a few hours, the glues would break down and the tanks would turn to mush. As Bob Sand recalls, "Planes were never landed with the paper tanks still aboard. Sometimes a mission was scrubbed soon after the group was airborne, and all forty-odd P-51s would swoop in single file over a dump on the field, releasing their tanks like a low level bombing mission. They would burst in a cloud of vapor, but by a miracle, none exploded. Here was 8,000 gallons of precious fuel being wasted. However, the tanks were too fragile to risk landing with, so it had to be done. We sure thought of the four gallons per week we were rationed for our cars back in the States!" This collection of tanks at Wormingford was just about enough for the 55th Fighter Group's P-51s to fly one mission. *Robert T. Sand*

withdraw, we would indirectly aid the bombers by preventing attack after we would normally leave. There is no set thumb rule as to how far you can leave the bombers because the tactics and the strategy of the situation are mentally weighed and thought out on the scene of the engagement and can never be predicted prior to a mission. . . .

Being on the offensive all of the time and attacking, although more than normal risk is involved, will give a Group higher scores and lower losses in any engagement, because aggressiveness on our part shakes the enemy to such a degree that he becomes excited and discouraged.

Mark E. Hubbard, *P–38 pilot, 20th Fighter Group*

Under no circumstances should there be less than two airplanes working together as one man cannot

Contrails in the sky above Wormingford on 11 December 1944. *Robert T. Sand*

Compared to their metal counterparts, paper drop tanks were light and easy to handle; just climb up the stack and toss them down. Unloading this batch are, left to right, S/Sgt. Robert G. Keich, Cpl. Howard Middlemas and Sgt. Michael H. Moran. *USAF/NASM*

protect his own tail, and 90% of all fighters shot down never saw the guy who hit them.

Walker M. Mahurin, *P-47 pilot, 56th Fighter Group*

In my opinion aerial combat isn't half of what it is shown to be in the movies. Most of us have some sort of an idea formed in our heads when we finally get into a combat theater. We like to think that the battle will assume proportions equal to those of the movies. You know how it is—one pilot sees the other, they both grit their teeth to beat hell, and finally the deadly combat begins with violent maneuvering by both parties. This field of thought is entirely erroneous. The combat usually takes place at a hell of a speed; the enemy plane is only seen for a few seconds. In nine cases out of ten the victor never sees his victim crash. As a result of the wrong idea, the new pilot first sees a Jerry ship, goes in to attack hell bent for election, and winds up feeling futile as the dickens. [I know] because I've done it myself many times. In fact, I've blown some darned good chances by just that sort of attack.

The conclusion I draw from this is that no combat is worthwhile unless the attacking pilot does his work in a very cool and calculating way. I don't do it that way myself, but I think that if I have got things pretty well figured out before I make a bounce, I stand a much better chance of bagging that guy I'm going down after. The cardinal points in an attack are first, be sure of your own position. See that

Mission planning in the operations hut. No one really liked to spend the long hours necessary, but it was absolutely vital to getting the job done. *USAF/NASM*

there are no Jerries around to make an attack on you. Secondly, make sure that you know what the Hun is doing. Try to figure out what you would do if you were in his position. Third, try to get up sun on him. This is extremely important, because once the element of surprise is lost the Jerry is about ten times as difficult to bring down. Even if he is not surprised, he still can't see into the sun—so the chances of getting

to him before he can make a turn are pretty darned good. Last, close right up his old rudder and let go. Then he'll be a dead Hun. Now, these are what I consider to be the most important points of combat, even though I don't [always] practice them myself, at least I try to.

Before I ever saw a Jerry, I used to spend hours just sitting in the old sack thinking up just exactly what I

would do if the Jerry were in such and such a position, and what I would do if he were doing something else. I think that it all paid in the long run. A couple of times I have been fortunate in running into just the situation I had dreamed of at one time or another. Then, I didn't have to think. I just acted, because I had mentally been in that very position before. I believe it helped. At least I would advocate it. I

Taxiing past the drop tank farm at Boxted, this 56th Fighter Group P–47D is ready to head for Germany as its crew chief looks on. *Mark H. Brown/USAFA*

still do it, and I hope that I run into a couple more of the dream castles, because it pays big dividends. At the same time, I don't always imagine what I would do if I were making the attack. I have it all figured out, also, when the Hun is on my tail. It can

happen anytime and sometimes has. I know that I don't consider the dreaming time wasted. It's a lot of fun, too.

In regard to looking behind and around, I realize that it is a subject that has been harped on by every guy

that has ever spent one measly hour on a combat operation. It is an absolute necessity. The result is most obvious. The Hun will never bag an American fighter if the Yank sees him coming in time to take proper evasive action. It is still a bad thing to spend

The 356th Fighter Group spread out and pulling contrails on long-range escort in early 1945. Tanks have not yet been dropped. *Herbert R. Rutland, Jr.*

Deep in Germany, 1945. A 356th Fighter Group P-51D on long-range escort has yet to drop its external tanks as pilots scan for enemy aircraft. *Herbert R. Rutland, Jr.*

130

all one's time looking behind. The idea behind fighter aircraft is that they will seek out the enemy and destroy him. A pilot will never accomplish this aim by looking behind him all the time. He must divide all his time to where it will do him the most good. If he knows that there are Huns above him, then, sure, look above and behind, but if he thinks the Hun is below him, then, for God's sake look in front and down. When you spot the Jerry go down and get him. Everyone knows about this subject so I think that I've said enough.

One thing that I believe should be stressed by all means is the reading of the mission reports of every group. Those daily summary reports that we get the next day after each mission are the most important of all the printed matter in our intelligence office. Both the bomber and fighter reports are good, because it is easy to see just what tactics the enemy has used against us. Also, it is easy to note just what changes have been made in previous days. I usually use this stuff to formulate some plan of attack that I would use if I were the German controller.

Sometimes it works. I know that I got my first victory from reading the mission reports turned in by Gene Roberts. On the day he first got a couple of Jerries, he put in the mission reports how the Jerry was lining up far out to the side and making head-on attacks on the bomber formation. Gene just happened to mention exactly how far away from the bombers the Jerries were. On August 17th [1943] I went out to the spot where Gene found his and I got two of them out there. Now, I'm a firm believer in the reports. So, I advocate

that all pilots read them. I kind of wish that accounts of the engagements were just a little more complete.

The next most important thing is the duty of all the positions in a squadron. I've been fortunate in that I have always been in a hitting position—leading a flight. I still think that it is the wingman who counts. I couldn't shoot down a thing if I were worrying about whether or not I had a wingman. He is the most important guy in the squadron. It is up to the wingman to cover his element leader no matter what. Sure, I know it's tough to sit back and tell a guy that he is clear behind so he can shoot down a Jerry. But look at it this way. Sooner or later the guy you're following around is going to be through with his tour. That'll leave a vacancy. The guy who will fill it will be the guy who has been giving the perfect job as a wingman. He will then get the chance to shoot, and probably will have profited by following a good shot around. Then, too, he will realize just what an important job the wingman has.

A good wingman is worth his weight in API [armor piercing incendiary ammunition]. So, for the wingmen, stick close to the man you fly with. Watch behind and let him look out in front. Fly well, and you will get to do all the shooting you want soon enough. I know I don't have to say a word about the leaders, because I've tried to beat all of them out of an attack from time to time, and it's almost impossible to get through the maze of Thunderbolts who have beaten me to the draw.

The last thing that I can stress is training. I think that my group probably does more training than any

other in the ETO. At least, it seems that way to me. I've been training ever since I got to the group and I imagine I'll continue to do so 'till the war is over. It really pays. Every worthwhile hour in the air is the most valuable thing I know of. After all, we are fighting for our lives. What's more, we are fighting for the most valuable thing in the world—Freedom. I think that these two things are well worth a little practice. Aerial camera gunnery is absolutely the most valuable training a man can get. Almost exactly like the real thing, only play with our own ships. Next in importance comes formation—both tactical and close. A good formation flyer will almost manufacture gasoline—something of which we don't have enough as it is. Third comes acrobatics, because a guy who knows what his airplane will do won't have to worry about how to make it do it when he could use the time shooting down a Hun. Fourth, anyone knows just how good a red-hot outfit looks when they take off and land. They really look good. This is all done by practice and don't think they don't feel proud of themselves when they do make good landings and take-offs. I know, because I'm in one of those red-hot outfits, and it makes me feel good as hell. The same old axiom applies:

"Anything worth doing is worth doing well."

Besides aerial camera work, I don't know of a thing that closely parallels shooting in combat. I certainly wish I did. My shooting is probably the worst in the whole Air Force. I know that most of us feel the same. Jerry Johnson is probably the best shot in the Air Force, but he

Capt. Robert Schmidt's *Tar Baby* cruises back home with the 356th Fighter Group after an escort mission. *Herbert R. Rutland, Jr.*

When pilots finished their tours and moved on, their aircraft were passed to successive pilots. Here Capt. Jack "Wild Bill" Crump flies the same aircraft Bob Schmidt named *Tar Baby*. Crump adorned the P-51 with a painting of his pet coyote, which flew several missions with him before being accidentally run over. *Herbert R. Rutland, Jr.*

Inbound to England from Germany, April 1945, 356th Fighter Group P-51Ds flown by Jack Crump, Nunzio B. Ceraolo and Don Jones are viewed from Herb Rutland's position as No. 2 in the flight. *Herbert R. Rutland, Jr.*

won't tell me how he does it. I have to get close enough to the Hun to reach out and club him before I can hit him. Usually, even that won't work. But, boy if I knew how to practice shooting, I would spend all my waking hours at it. If we, and I speak of the Air Forces as a whole, could only shoot perfectly we would double our score with no effort at all. When the man does come forth who has invented a way of simulating combat, complete with shooting down the target, then we will win the air war hands down.

Hubert "Hub" Zemke, *P-47 pilot, 56th Fighter Group*

A fighter pilot must possess an inner urge to do combat. The will at all times to be offensive will develop into his own tactics. . . .

Learn to break at the proper time to make a head-on attack. The enemy doesn't like it. Don't run. That's just what he wants you to do. He can't help from getting right behind you if you are moving away. When caught by the enemy in large force the best policy is to fight like hell until you can decide what to do next.

V. K. Meroney, *P-47 pilot, 352nd Fighter Group*

When we get replacements, they know practically nothing of the many

Before the pilot can get out of his Mustang at Wormingford, 55th Fighter Group personnel climb up and gather around to hear what the Christmas Eve 1944 mission to Germany was like. From left to right, Sergeant Woods (assistant crew chief), Lieutenant Miller (engineering officer), Lieutenant Grimmer (communications officer), Master Sergeant Stone (flight chief) and, at bottom, Zuckerman (radio man). *Robert T. Sand*

things that go towards making a good fighter pilot. Their training, before we get them, is a headache in itself; what with all the safety precaution and all that they have back in the States. . . .

I believe the main things are . . . teamwork . . . confidence in your leaders, your ships, and that old fighting heart.

Kill the bastards!!!

John C. Meyer, *P-47 pilot, 352nd Fighter Group*

Showing a willingness to fight often discourages the Hun even when he outnumbers us, while on the other hand I have, by immediately breaking for the deck on other occasions, given the Hun a "shot in the arm," turning his half-hearted attack into an aggressive one.

I do not like the deck. This is especially true in the Pas-de-Calais area [in northern France]. I believe that it may be used effectively to avoid an area of numerically superior E/A [enemy aircraft] because of the difficulty in seeing an aircraft on the deck from above. With all silver planes this excuse is even doubtful. The danger from small arms fire especially near the coast is great. I realize that I differ from some of my contemporaries in this respect, but two thirds of our Squadron losses have been from enemy small arms fire. . . . When an aircraft is below 8,000 feet over enemy territory, it [should] be just as low as possible. Twenty feet above the ground is too high. . . .

I am not a good shot. Few of us are. To make up for this I hold my fire until I have a shot of less than 20 degrees deflection and until I'm within 300 yards. Good discipline on this score can make up for a great deal.

Robert S. Johnson, *P-47 pilot, 56th Fighter Group*

A lot of green pilots fly good combat formation for the first, second or third mission. If they see no enemy, many of them get cocky and think combat is a cinch. They relax and maybe get away with it several trips over enemy territory—then it happens. The first enemy they see or have contact with knocks them down, simply because they didn't see the enemy. They were too relaxed to kick the airplane rudders or roll the ship up on a wing and look behind and above them as well as straight ahead or at their leaders. It's much easier and better to come home tired with a sore neck from looking constantly in every direction and being tired from constantly skidding sideways to look behind and around you than it is to leave the thing you *sit on* over enemy territory. Once in a while it's good business to put a wing tip up just over the sun and look around it too. Often there is plenty of company there.

Never let a Jerry get his sights on you. No matter whether he is at 100 yards or 1,000 yards away, 20 mm will carry easily that far and will

Back from what turned out to be the biggest mission of the war, 24 December 1944, with 2,046 bombers and 853 fighters sent out against targets in western Germany, pilots of the 55th Fighter Group listen on the ramp at Wormingford as Lieutenant Koenig tries to describe what it was like. The no smoking near aircraft rule was routinely broken under the pressure of wartime flying. *Robert T. Sand*

A pilot and navigator, 94th Bomb Group, check their watches before takeoff. *Robert T. Sand*

easily knock down a plane at 1,000 yards. It is better to stay at 20,000 feet, than it is to pull up in his vicinity at a stalling speed. If he comes down on you pull up into him and 9 times out of 10, if you are nearly head-on with him he'll roll away to his right.

Then you have him. Roll on to his tail and go get him. If he tries to turn with you and can out turn you, pull the nose up straight ahead and kick rudder and stick toward him and you can slice to the inside of him. The enemy thinks then that you are turning

inside him and tries to dive away and outrun your bullets!

Try this and any other trick you think of in friendly combat.

Anytime you lose your wing man or leader, you've lost 75% of your eyes and fighting strength. Jerries will

Field maintenance on the 94th Bomb Group's *Mighty Mike* at Bury St. Edmonds. Ground crews at bomber bases had a massive job in keeping aircraft combat ready, and much of the work was performed in the open at the assigned hardstand. Only the seriously damaged aircraft were pulled into the hangars. *Byron Trent*

135

shoot at anyone. Never think you're a favorite to them. Anyone can get it, some of the best have gotten it. So keep your eyes open.

Harry J. Dayhuff, *P-47 pilot, 78th*
Fighter Group

If the Hun is right on your tail do something quick and violent. (As one of our pilots once said when the first he was aware of a Hun were the tracers going by his shoulder, "I put the stick in one corner and the rudder in the other. I don't know what happened but when I came out the Hun wasn't there any longer.")

If outnumbered, dive like hell (that is in a Thunderbolt—other fighter types may prefer other methods).

If the Hun is in shooting range always keep the ball going in each corner—never give him an opportunity to line up his sights. Remember this slows you up though. . . .

Most successful offensive actions come with superior speed and altitude coupled with surprise. Always use the sun or blind spots to obtain surprise.

Duane W. Beeson, *P-51 pilot, 4th*
Fighter Group

I think the most important one thing to a fighter pilot is speed! The faster an aircraft is moving when he spots an enemy aircraft, the sooner he will be able to take the bounce and get to the Hun. And it's harder for him to bounce you if you are going fast. . . .

Never give the Hun an even break. If you have any advantage on him, keep it and use it. So, when attacking, I would say, plan to

136

overshoot him if possible; hold fire until within range, then shoot and clobber him down to the last instant before breaking away. It's sorta like sneaking up behind and hitting him with a baseball bat.

Official AAF History

It is difficult to escape the conclusion that the air battles did more to defeat the Luftwaffe than did the destruction of the aircraft factories.

Arthur L. Thorsen, *P-38 pilot, 55th*
Fighter Group

The briefing room was large, but it was filled to capacity. All of the chairs were occupied and there were some small groups, standing. They must have gotten everyone up for this briefing, I thought. Someone said, "Don't tell me they're gonna' send us on a 'do' in this soup! I had to go on instruments just to walk over here!" This was greeted with good-natured, but weak laughter.

As the intelligence and weather officers gathered at the dais, I looked over the scores of pilots who were engrossed in animated chatter. It was easy, I thought, to tell the veterans from the beginners. You could recognize them by their eyes. Veterans' eyes were surrounded by wrinkled and sunburned flesh. They all appeared to be wearing tan bandits' masks. Below the eyes and where the oxygen masks covered the lower halves of their faces, the flesh was white. On the other hand, pilots fresh from the States had pink, unwrinkled faces. In the briefing room now, the veterans seemed to outnumber the beginners, but not by much.

I suddenly realized I was studying the faces of the men more intently with each briefing. It was as if I didn't know who was coming back again and wanted that one last look to remember them by. I shook myself, fighting a wave of depression. I hated being maudlin.

Maj. Todd Crowell of Headquarters Squadron, standing at the back of the room suddenly barked "Ten-hut!" and everyone came out of their chairs to stand at attention. Everyone that is, except Don Penn. He didn't know how. Shepard maintained that Penn really knew how to stand at attention, it was always his clothes that were 'at ease.' Now Colonel [Jack] Jenkins called out "At ease!" and stepped up on the dais.

The men relaxed, but did not sit down. Jenkins turned and faced them, studying the expressions on the faces of the pilots gathered there. Finally, he said, quietly, "Be seated, gentlemen." There was a shuffling of feet as the men resumed their seats. Jenkins turned, picked up a pointer and stepped to the red curtain covering the wall map. Quickly he drew the curtain aside and one could see the crimson ribbon stretching from our field at Nuthampstead to deep in Germany. There was a low, but audible mass intake of breath followed by a score or more of loose bowels. The target was Berlin!

Colonel Jenkins began speaking. "Your eyes aren't playing tricks on you gentlemen," he said, "The target is Berlin! Right in Hitler's back yard!" He tapped Berlin with the pointer and continued, "The weather is pretty foul, but I'm sure we can get through. We'll have full belly tanks, but we'll want to fly pretty lean all the way in, just to make sure. We're flying target support, so if we're engaged and have to dump tanks, we won't make rendezvous and that won't be too good for our 'Big Friends.'

"This is a maximum effort and fighters from all the other groups will be participating, either with us on target support, or escort on penetration or withdrawal. So look sharp! Most of the planes up there will be ours. Don't shoot any of them down!" A sprinkling of chuckles filled the room as Jenkins continued. "Takeoff will be at 0930 . . . rendezvous at 1200. Tom will give you the lowdown now on what you may expect."

Maj. Tom Welch, chief of the intelligence group, got to his feet and took the pointer from Jenkins. "Well, boys," he began, "this one's a doozy. If you don't get a little excitement out of this one, you're not really trying. Our intelligence reports are that the Jerries have moved more 88s into the Amsterdam area, so you'll get more

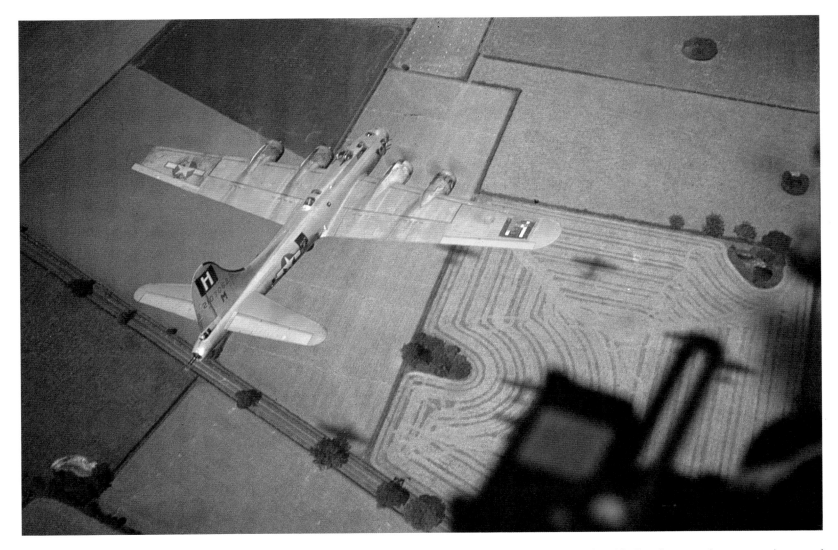

The lead B-17 of the 388th Bomb Group takes the formation home to Knettishall after attacking Brest, France, 26 August 1944. The "Big Friends" flew into the roughest of conditions and the wear and tear was evident on their aircraft. This Fort has a replacement wing panel from a camouflaged sister ship, deeply stained engine nacelles and flaking paint. *Mark H. Brown/USAFA*

than the usual amount of flak going in. It'll get heavier here at Hanover." He tapped both places with his pointer, "More at Stendal and everything including the toilet seat at Berlin itself. Going in, you'll probably encounter fighters here at Hanover." He tapped the spot with his pointer. "Look for them again at Oschersleben and Brunswick. Be sure to check out escape kits with your squadrons before you go. Any questions?"

"Yes sir!" A tall, gangly pilot from the 338th Squadron stood up. "What about some good news?" he asked.

"Certainly," replied Welch, "Spam sandwiches for all when you return! Good luck!" With that he handed the pointer to the Weather Officer and sat down. So did [the] gangly pilot from the 338th.

Jenkins again: "Gentlemen, as you can easily see outside, the weather stinks, so don't lose sight of the flights up ahead of you on takeoff, or we'll never form up. For more on the weather problem, here's our weather merchant."

There were scattered boos and hisses as the weather officer made his report.

"Visibility is down to a little more than a half mile," he said, "so you won't see the end of the runway. It should improve some when you come back. The stuff thins out at 18,000 feet and you should be in the clear by 20,000 feet. Temperature at 20,000, minus 52 degrees. The soup should taper off by the time you reach Osnabruck, with bright sunshine and unlimited visibility the rest of the way to the target. This is indeed an instrument mission, gentlemen, but I

138

see no icing conditions." He was given a round of boos as he sat down.

Colonel Jenkins came forward again. We synchronized watches and he said, "We'll form up at 5,000 feet before we head out. That's all gentlemen. Good luck!"

Taking off . . . was a bit hairy. One no sooner got his wheels up when the ground began to disappear in the fog. We began a slow, climbing turn to the left, forsaking the more colorful peel-up of clearer days. My eyes moved continuously between my instruments and Captain Wyche's ship, for I was flying his wing again. I could barely discern ships just ahead and those who took off first were swallowed up completely in the deadly mist. In school we were never taught to fly a tight formation in this stuff. It would have sent air safety officers screaming to their mistresses, for comfort.

The weather wrapped around us like a fuzzy cocoon. It was like flying through a bottle of milk. Soon we were at 5,000 feet. Then 10,000. I snapped on my oxygen mask. Berlin! Gay Berlin! Will we ever get there to dance the oom-pah-pah on the Reichstag? The radio was silent. Good discipline. If anyone was spinning in, he wasn't telling the others about it. Silence, save for the drone of the engines. They sounded good and I blessed my crew chief, Sergeant Harmon. I chanced a look through the windscreen. Nothing. We were in a ghostly purgatory waiting for something to happen.

How many hours will it take to fly through this stuff? How do we find the ground when we get back home? Drone, drone! The engines still sounded good. I wondered if others

were having mechanical difficulties. I looked at my altimeter, 24,000 feet! What did old Lieutenant Cold Front say? We'd be in the clear by 20,000 feet? How can you tell that by wetting your finger and sticking it out the window? 24,000 feet and the stuff was as thick as ever. The engines droned sweetly. If we didn't see land soon, they would put me to sleep. I looked at my wrist watch. 1055. We should be crossing in at The Hague now. Better brace yourself for a flak barrage, I told myself. But nothing happened. The minutes ticked by. It was 1130. No flak, no anything. We were flying in a void, detached from the world. I checked my altimeter. We had climbed to 30,000 feet and we were still in the soup. I felt a slight touch of vertigo. I shook myself and began to sing. It was another little RAF ditty I had picked up in some vile den.

The minstrels sing of an
    English King, that lived many
    years ago
He ruled his land with an iron
    hand, but his mind was weak
    and low.
He loved to hunt the royal stag
    that roamed the royal wood,
But better he loved the pleasure
    of—pulling his royal pud.
All hail the bastard king of
    England.

It was a rather foul song, but it gave me comfort. Drone, drone! The engines were accompanying me. By the time I got to, "The Queen of Spain was a glamorous dame and an amorous dame was she," vertigo left me, so I abandoned the wretched song. I looked at my wristwatch. 1145. We should be making rendezvous soon, but what good would it do? You couldn't find your behind with both hands in this solid soup.

Suddenly we broke clear, into sunny unlimited visibility. It was like being thrown off a cliff. We popped out of the muck and there was a 30,000 foot drop to the ground below us. There were only a few P–38s in front of us and one behind. Where in hell did they all go? Then on my right and left, other P–38s popped into the clear and began assembling around us. I looked behind me. The other two ships of our flight were not there. I counted those that were. Sixteen. Only sixteen of us got through. Sixteen out of 45 that started and there wasn't a bomber in sight.

My nerves were pushed almost beyond endurance from the long instrument flight . . . my imagination had me colliding with another P–38. . . . [After spotting some 110s and 190s we] once again picked up a heading for England, plunging into the wall of stratocumulus that obliterated the continent. Back on instruments again . . . all the way to England and Nuthampstead. When we arrived at 1500 hours, the field was socked in and we circled, trying to find it through the muck. Then someone on the ground with a high I.Q. dispatched a jeep-load of flare shells and two enlisted men with pistols to the end of the field where they took up positions on each side of the runway and proceeded to fire flares straight up. Beautiful! We could see the flares. All we had to do was land between the two flare pistols popping off, methodically. Everyone landed safely.

Glenn T. Eagleston, *P–51 pilot, 354th Fighter Group*

We were all pretty aroused at the debriefing. We were happy that this milestone was past and we had gone in and bombed hell out of the German capital, we thought at the time, without too much loss to ourselves. In all we went to Berlin four times that week and I've never been so tired in my life—6 hour missions one right after the other just knocked the 'coon pee right out of you. I'd swear I could have given you the serial number off my oxygen bottle and dinghy pack by reading it off my left cheek.

Bert Stiles, *B–17 copilot, 91st Bomb Group (from his book* Serenade to the Big Bird, *W. W. Norton & Co., 1952)*

We were like old men. It seemed like the sun had gone out of the world. I looked in the mirror and a haggard mask of a face stared back at me. The eyes were bright. And the veins were cleanly etched in the whites, and the pupils were distended. We were all like that. "I'm gonna get grounded," Sam said. "They're trying to kill us off."

We'd been in the group twelve days. The first four days we did

The 493rd Bomb Group's B–24s line up for takeoff from Debach in the summer of 1944. *Mark. H. Brown/USAFA*

nothing. The next eight, we flew. Grant had a thin face anyway, but by then it was like an ax. Bird was impossible to get along with; neither of them could sleep.

I could sleep. Or maybe it was a form of death. I would stretch out in my sack and feel my muscles give way completely. There was no pleasure in it. They just went flat and lifeless. And then my nerve endings would die for a while, until Porada came to wake us up.

"Breakfast at two. Briefing at three." He was always nice about it. Quiet and easy and insistent.

I would lie there and the glare of the light would smash back into my mind. Somewhere in the Reich today. Somewhere in that doomed land. There was a movie named *Each Dawn I Die*. It was like that.

After I got my clothes on, and out into the night, it was better. I'd stand still and look away at the stars and ask Lady Luck to bring me back

home. Just ask her. Just hoped she'd stay with me another day. One day at a time. Taking one day at a time we got through it.

Don Larson, *C-47 pilot, 444th Troop Carrier Group*

I've lost all conception of time lately. Between working all nights planning these missions, flying most of the day, and listening to the British government switch from Greenwich to British Standard to British Summer to

Old Baldy sits in its 486th Bomb Group revetment at Sudbury while being serviced for the next day's mission. *Mark H. Brown/USAFA*

This 490th Bomb Group B-24 is in the process of being brought up to operational status for the next mission. Bombs have been "dropped" off onto the ground for loading into the open bomb bays. They also make handy bike stands. Deicer boots on the leading edges of the wings have been removed for summer flying. *Mark H. Brown/USAFA*

View across the 490th Bomb Group bomb dump at Eye Peninsula. These 1,000 pound and 500 pound general purpose bombs await loading into the Group's Forts. *Mark H. Brown/USAFA*

Double British Summer Time, and then back down the scale—I usually didn't even know the date or month.

Well, I guess you've read about the "commitment of the first airborne army." Mostly, I still can't talk about it—but as the communiques say, I lost "some" friends. My crew chief, for whom I have a great deal of affection, as we've been together since Sedalia, was badly wounded.

One oil tank, hydraulic tank, electric system and all radios were shot up, to say nothing of forty-something holes, one as big as a baseball bat, right through my roof. Oh, yes, my side window was smashed, about three inches from my

head, and that, too, somehow missed me. I wasn't scared though—Haw! Two days later, when they quieted me down, I told 'em just what happened.

So many things happened there in such a short time that it seems like a bad dream. In fact, one of the radio operators talked about "flak sandwiches" all that night in his sleep.

I know now for certain that when the pressure is really on you fly by instinct alone. Once, when we were hit, my co-pilot and I were both flying the ship 'cause we *knew* the other one was dead, yet we were unaware of the other's pressure on the controls. When you watch the formation ahead of you getting hell, ships crazily burning,

spiraling, exploding, knowing that in a fraction of a second it will be shifted on you, it brings on a feeling that cannot be described as mere fear—it paralyzes the brains, turns muscles to jelly—and God and instinct alone take care of man.

I now have personal effects scattered with rear echelons in Italy, France, and two bases in England—that is also why mail never finds us—can't catch up with us. A.T.C. [Air Transport Command] brings the mail, and when A.T.C. catches up with the troop carrier it will be 'cause the war's over and there's nowhere left to go. Told you that A.T.C. stands for "Allergic to Combat," didn't I?

The 100th Bomb Group has just returned to Thorpe Abbots from Germany—with casualties. The "meat wagon", was on the scene quickly as engines were shut down and the wounded offloaded. *Mark H. Brown/USAFA*

142

Robert Shoens, *B-17 pilot, 100th*
Bomb Group

Somewhere over France one of the crew asked, "Has anyone seen our escort lately?" Suddenly it was obvious that no one had. The chatter stopped. You could feel the tension rise. It wasn't long before there appeared ahead of us what looked like a swarm of bees, fighters several miles off but coming at us, dozens of them. It became obvious in a few seconds that we were their target as they came straight at us. It apparently didn't bother them that our greatest fire power was straight ahead. In an instant they went right through us. In that instant eight of nine planes in the high squadron were gone. The group lead aircraft had a six foot gap in his vertical stabilizer.

As pilot you don't see much; you are busy keeping your aircraft in position, but a glance through the overhead window told me the high squadron was gone. On our right wing was a crew from our barracks. Their

A 486th Bomb Group B-17G climbs out over England in the spring of 1945. The war was almost over but the Big Friends continued to hammer the German war machine. *Alexander C. Sloan via Bob Kuhnert, 355th FG Assn.*

143

entire wing was on fire. Before they could get out, there was nothing there. By the end of the third attack we were all alone! One aircraft from the entire group? It couldn't be, yet, there we were.

As we circled the field after getting home we could see a lot of empty spaces and we knew we were at least one of the few. We landed and when we taxied to our space, we found our squadron commander waiting for us. He was crying. We were stunned to learn that we were the only aircraft to return to the field and only one of four to make it back to England out of the original group of 20 aircraft. Of the 8th Air Force aircraft lost over Germany that day we had lost almost 25% of them. What do you say, what do you do when your squadron commander is crying and wants to know what happened? You do the same thing he is doing.

Stanley A. Hutchins, *B-24 pilot, 484th Bomb Group*

I desperately tried to transfer into P-38s and did everything that a 19 year old could think of to shake B-24 dust off my feet. Tolerantly the 15th Air Force said fine, just finish your bomber tour first. The B-24, and my escapist attitude toward it, ruined my "feel" so that it took 10 hours of dual to check me out in an AT-6 in July 1945. I am grudgingly grateful to the B-24 for bringing me home over those 11 months in combat, still I never got to live my dream of rat racing an Me 109 into the ground.

Robert E. Kuhnert, *radio line chief, 335th Fighter Group*

Ward Douglass, forming up with the 358th Fighter Squadron one day in the familiar base-circling pattern, accidentally dropped a full wing tank directly over Bassingbourn Airdrome. The tank went through the mess hall

roof, spraying avgas throughout the kitchen. Luckily, there were no casualties. The 91st Bomb Group C.O. sent the following cryptic message to our 355th Group C.O.: "We are not the enemy."

James R. Hanson, *P-51 pilot, 339th Fighter Group*

Knowing that we are now headed out for the real thing, for the first time, is beyond description. We circle the field to get everyone into set course formation. It's a beautiful, sunny day with about 3/10ths clouds at about 8,000 feet. It's a great feeling to look around the formation, knowing who is in each plane, guys you've flown with and lived with in the States and now together doing the job you were trained for and in the airplane you had hoped to fly.

Crossing out over the North Sea, Col. Hayes calls, "Oilskin, feet are wet." I know that a lot of us are

The 388th Bomb Group has just returned to Knettishall from bombing Brest on 26 August 1944 and ground crews are already servicing and refueling this Flying Fort, the lead ship of the high squadron that day. *Mark H. Brown/USAFA*

taking a long look at the beautiful green English countryside, thinking that it is going to be home from now on. We climb steadily on up to 20,000 feet. Up ahead I can see the French and Belgian coast. We make landfall near Dunkirk. I've read enough about that place. The sky is clear and blue and the land below looks so green and peaceful with those scattered, puffy clouds . . . then wham bang, it's flak at 7 o'clock. There it is for the first time . . . doesn't look dangerous . . . just appears like magic, black and umbrella shaped, fading away quickly to a gray smoke as it drifts back behind. We make some evasive turns and nothing really comes close to us but I really get a stab of excitement each time I hear that call of "Flak!"

Back to the hardstand, this 490th Bomb group B-17G heads down the taxiway at Eye after turning off the active runway upon completion of another trip over enemy territory. *Mark H. Brown/USAFA*

Terre Haute Tornado, a B-26 Marauder of the 344th Bomb Group, at rest in England. Generally speaking, fighter pilots found escorting Marauders and A-26 Invaders to be far easier than escorting the heavy four-engine types. This was due primarily to equal cruising speeds, which eliminated the fighters having to weave over the bomber formation. *Mark H. Brown/USAFA*

145

Chapter 8

Huns

Ernst Schroeder, *Fw 190 pilot,*
Jagdgeschwader 300

I catch sight of the glittering reflections of the sun on the uncamouflaged American bombers, off to the left and at the same altitude, about 25,000 feet. Still a long way away, the stately enemy formation crosses in front of us from left to right. I carefully search the sky for enemy escorts, but I can make out only three or four condensation trails above the bombers.

Curving round, the Sturmgruppe is now directly in front of me, about

Though several different aircraft were manufactured by Willy Messerschmitt's company, the use of his name among Americans usually meant a single machine, the Me 109. Built in multiple versions, 109s flew in combat from the Spanish Civil War through the end of World War II, giving Allied pilots a rough time when flown by skilled pilots. "Black 12," an Me 109 G-10/R2, flew with 2./NAG 14 at the end of the war. *Ralph Woolner via Monogram Aviation Publications*

150 yards below; I have a grandstand view of the attack as it unfolds. The bombers open up with a furious defensive fire, filling the sky with tracers as we move in at full throttle. At 300 yards the main body of the Fw 190s opens up with their 20 mm and 30 mm cannon, the murderous trains of high explosive shells streaking out towards the Liberators. Within seconds two of the giant aircraft have exploded into great fireballs, while several others have caught fire and are falling out of formation.

On either side of me my Schwarm comrades fire like mad and score hit after hit on their targets. Looking around, I see the sky is like a

When pilots in the MTO encountered Me 109s, it did not follow that they were necessarily flown by Germans. Several Italian *Regia Aeronautica* units were equipped with 109s and flown throughout the war against the Allies. This Me 109 G–6/trop at Sciacca, Sicily was attached to the 365ª Squadriglia, 150° Gruppo until the Italian capitulation on 8 September 1943. *William J. Skinner*

An Fw 190 G–3, fighter-bomber version of the famous Focke-Wulf, sits at Montecorvino Airfield, near Salerno, Italy in 1943. *William J. Skinner*

chaotic circus: whirling and fluttering pieces of aircraft, an entire wing falling complete with engines and propellers still turning, several parachutes and some of our aircraft battling with the few P-38 escort fighters that have reached us.

Arthur L. Thorsen, *P-38 pilot, 55th Fighter Group*

I was turning tight with the German now and my ship trembled and buffeted slightly. I couldn't pull enough deflection on him, but I had him, he had no place to go. He couldn't dive and if he climbed, he was finished. All he could do was try to out turn me. We could turn like this forever, I thought and quickly dumped ten percent flaps. My ship reared up and turned on its wingtip. I was out turning the Jerry. I opened fire and saw strikes around the cockpit and left wing root. The thrill of the chase is hypnotic. Your body tingles. You feel you have wings of your own. You make funny noises to yourself. You strain against your shoulder straps as if that will give you more momentum. You begin to tremble with the knowledge that the German ship ahead of you, is yours. You can take him. You don't think of shooting a human being, you just shoot at a machine. Air combat is strictly that impersonal.

The German was not done yet and rolled out quickly to starboard, sucking in his stick and pulling vapor streamers from his wing tips. I rolled with him, but he had me by a second and I lost my deflection. We were in a vertical turn now and the centrifugal force was pushing me hard into the seat. I was about 150 yards astern of him when his ship filled my gun sight. I pulled through and opened fire. I could see strikes on his engine and pieces flew off. Then a long stream of glycol poured from his engine and I knew he was finished. He suddenly pulled out of the turn, went into a steep climb, popped his canopy and bailed out. We were very low, almost too low for bailing out. I followed him down and his chute must have popped just as his feet hit the ground.

I began a series of turns to clear my tail and couldn't see an airplane in the sky. Then I noticed, as I was turning at low level, scores of Parisians dancing around the roof tops and throwing their berets in the air, as if cheering what they had been watching. I chuckled as I turned the nose of my ship toward home.

Heinz Knoke, *Me 109 pilot, Jagdgeschwader 11*

I jumped into the cockpit for my second mission of the day. The mechanics climbed up on the right

A deadly opponent, this Focke-Wulf Fw 190 D-9 flew with II./JG 6 as "Black 12," in 1945. An upgraded version of the radial-engined 190, the "Dora 9," had an inline liquid-cooled V-12 engine with a circular radiator in front, giving it the nickname "long nose" in both American and German squadrons. In all respects the 190 D-9 was the equal of its American counterpart, the P-51D. *Ralph Woolner via Monogram Aviation Publications*

wing with the heavy starting handle and began winding up the inertia starter. As I sat there in the cockpit, canopy open, the nose pointing north, I noticed two aircraft coming straight for me from the east, very low. American fighters! I threw off my straps and scrambled out of the cockpit, shouting "Tiefangriff!" to the two mechanics. They were not quick enough, just standing there looking around, while I was already out of my 109 and diving into a small ditch nearby. Finally Kretchmer jumped down, a few steps behind me, but the second mechanic was still standing on the wing, looking to see what was happening.

At that moment the bullets started flying all around us. The aircraft was hit several times, with six or seven holes in and around the cockpit . . . the canopy was smashed. Then I heard the cries from the second mechanic. He lost three fingers from his right hand and had one shot through his buttock. Then the Mustangs flashed close overhead at 20 meters and were away—I could see their muzzle flashes. . . .

Shortly after 2200 I got on my bicycle and pedaled in the darkness the one and a half kilometers from the

Though less maneuverable than single engined fighters, the Messerschmitt 110 had to be approached with care if a skilled gunner manned the rear seat. This Me 110 G-2 of II/2G 1 at Montecorvino, Italy, 1943, is painted in the unit's colorful *Wespe* (wasp) insignia. *William J. Skinner*

airfield to the small guesthouse where my wife and infant daughter were staying. It was a funny kind of war. Each evening I went home to my wife.

She was asleep and I think I was a little bit drunk when I got there. I just got undressed and climbed into bed with my wife. Sleepily she turned around and said, "Hey, are you drunk? What have you been up to?" I said, "We've had a lot of work." She rolled over and went back to sleep. I was up before she awoke—had to be at the Staffel between 5 and 6 AM.

That day had been one of the most exciting, exhausting and frightening day's fighting I had ever had. I had battled with fighters, knocked down a bomber, made a crash-landing on one wheel, been in a plane shot up on the ground, lost one of our ground crewmen wounded, gone into action a second time, lost my wingman, returned to base and got drunk.

John B. Murphy, *P-51 pilot, 359th Fighter Group*

My first impression when I saw the jet plane was that I was standing still. It seemed hopeless to try to attempt to overtake them, but my actions were prompted by a curiosity to get as close to them as possible. I believe that will be the reaction of every pilot that comes in contact with them.

Hermann Greiner, *Me 110 pilot, Nacht Jagdgeschwader 1*

Just as I got airborne after being scrambled, I could hardly believe my eyes. There, at a height of 200 meters (100 above me), a B-17 was flying straight towards me with two fighters flying loose escort. I pulled the stick back, made a steep turn to the left and opened fire at it right away, even before I had time to retract my landing gear and flaps, which put me

on the edge of my Messerschmitt's capabilities. With so little speed, there was grave danger that my machine would stall out and fall into a spin. As I held my plane on the edge of a stall and fired, the Fortress was so badly hit that it was forced to make a belly landing. The enemy fighters were then closing in so I had to dive under them, get into my own airfield's flak defenses and land to escape. Later I found out that six or seven of the ten Americans in the bomber had escaped without injury.

Walter Hagenah, *Fw 190 pilot, Jagdgeschwader 3*

To be sure of bringing down a bomber it was essential that we held our fire until we were right up close against the bombers. We were to advance like Frederick the Great's infantrymen, holding our fire until we could see "the white of the enemy's eyes."

One of the most potent German aircraft of the war, the Messerschmitt Me 262 jet fighter presented a real challenge to AAF fighter pilots. Fortunately a combination of tactics and numbers allowed Mustang units to engage and down 262s on a regular basis, though when the jets did get through to the bombers they proved to be extremely effective. This EJG 2 aircraft sits at Lechfeld in 1945. *Byron Trent*

Chapter 9

On the Deck

Frances H. Griswold, *CO, VIII Fighter Command*

Since the beginning of this war the profit and loss on the proposition of fighter aircraft attacking ground targets has been the subject of professional debate and pilot discussion. Small profit to shoot up two or three trucks or a couple of machine guns for the loss of a valuable aircraft and pilot. Worse still when two, three, four go down over one well-dispersed enemy A/D [airdrome] or, as on the days of our large-scale attacks by the whole

A 313th Fighter Squadron, 50th Fighter Group Thunderbolt just about to touch down at Nancy, France, in the winter of 1944. In spite of the rough weather conditions on the Continent, Ninth AF aircraft operated continually in support of the First and Third Armies. *Phil Savides*

Amidst the bare base rubble at Nancy, France, the ground crew of Phil Savides' 50th Fighter Group P–47D *Juicy Lucy* gets things ready for the next mission. The Ninth Air Force turned the Thunderbolt into the finest ground attack weapon on the Allied side under the leadership of Gen. Elwood "Pete" Quesada. *Phil Savides*

Command, twenty-five or more may be MIA [missing in action]. In addition to the loss of these planes and pilots is the unfortunate fact that our best, our outstanding leaders and fighters who had yet to meet their match in any enemy they could see, have gone down before the hidden gunfire or light flak incident to a ground attack. Duncan, Beeson, Beckham, Gerald Johnson, Gabreski, Juchheim, Andrew, Hofer, Goodson, Schreiber, Millikan, Carpenter, the list could go on.

For equal numbers engaged, four times as many pilots of this Command are lost on ground attack as in aerial combat. Light flak will ring an A/D [airdrome] or an M/Y [marshalling yard]. Flak cars will open up in the middle of a train. A truck convoy, with sufficient warning, may be a hornet's nest. Every target of special value to the enemy will be heavily defended and may exact its price.

Where then is the profit? The answer is the successful invasion and the victorious battle of France. The answer is our flight of many a heavy bomber mission without challenge by enemy fighters, and the presence of our hordes of bombers and fighter-bombers over our troops in Normandy. The roads of France, strewn with enemy wreckage, reply, and an enemy starving for oil, ammunition, supplies, reinforcement could answer with deep feeling.

Donald J.M. Blakeslee, *P-51 pilot, CO, 4th Fighter Group*
I use terrain—hills, gullies, and trees—for cover, and such airdrome installations as hangars, etc., to screen my approach. I never come right in on an airdrome if I can help it. If I have

154

planned to attack an airdrome beforehand, I pick an I.P. [initial point] some 10 miles away—some easily recognizable place. I have my course from there to the drome worked out. Once in the air, I take my boys right past the airdrome as if I had no intention of attacking it at all. At my I.P. I let down and swing back flat on the deck. I usually try to have another check-point on the course from my I.P., not far from the airdrome, and when I pass that I know I am definitely coming in on the right field. I don't like to end up on an airdrome before I realize I am even coming to one. But once I hit the drome, I really get down on the deck. I don't mean five feet up; I mean so low the grass is brushing the bottom of the scoop.

After the attack on the field, stay on the deck for a good mile beyond the drome before pulling up. The break should consist of rudder yawing. Never cock a wing up. If you must turn on the drome, do flat skidding turns. Don't give the Hun a better target to shoot at.

I prefer to get down low and shoot up at any aircraft on the ground rather than come in high and shoot down. Usually I fire a short burst from long range and correct for it as I come in.

In general, my pilots and I realize ground strafing involves a greater risk than shooting Huns down in the air. But it seems to be quite as important. Besides, we get more fun out of strafing ground targets instead of airfields—no one really likes to attack these.

I want to say a word about tactics. My feeling is that there is entirely too much emphasis placed on

methods of strafing and on so-called tactics. Strafing is a simple process. You pick a target and shoot it up. As long as you are comfortable and get away with it, that's all there is to it. Every pilot probably has a different idea on how to do it. A general rule just can't be laid down, for one method is probably no better than another.

Philip Savides, *P-47 pilot, 50th Fighter Group*
Juicy Lucy was a hand-me-down P-47 which I received without question just as a poor kid puts on the jacket of his older brother. No one told me who was the previous pilot nor did I ever ask about him. The plane outlasted the war, I believe, but I left Europe without saying goodbye to her.

In my recollections, we (or at least I) often flew different planes. It seems to me that even after I was assigned *Juicy Lucy* I frequently flew other aircraft, although she was ready for flight. Why that should be, I cannot explain. Maybe, because I was easy going and did not demand or reject certain aircraft, *Lucy* was assigned to another pilot on some flights while I found myself in the one which he, for some whim, found unacceptable.

In spite of what might appear to be a disinterest in a particular P-47, I developed an enduring affection for the breed. Sure, there was that obvious obesity coupled with a drinking problem and the undeniable fact that she glided like a flat iron and looked—head on—like a flying toilet seat. Yet, I'm grateful for the chance I had to pilot the Thunderbolt. It was a mighty fine, mighty machine.

Thomas J.J. Christian, Jr., *P-51 pilot, CO, 361st Fighter Group*

Usually, a successful fighter attack against a ground target requires less skill, more nerve, and as precise an estimate of the situation as an air-to-air attack. We say *usually* because there are exceptions; for example, successful fighter-bombing is a specialized sport which requires considerable practice and skill; moreover, it does not take any courage to shoot up an undefended target (provided that you know beforehand that the target *is* undefended); and, it is often much easier to make a proper estimate of a ground situation than it is to make one of an air situation because, in many cases, we are afforded prior knowledge of the target conditions.

The latter is never true in air-to-air combat.

Ben Rimerman, *P-47 pilot, CO, 353rd Fighter Group*

A few main points to remember are that a definite target should always be selected before the approach to the attack should be made. The target should be worth what you have to pay, meaning that it is foolish to lead a flight into a heavily defended airdrome to shoot up an old, beat-up Fieseler Storch if that is all you can see. Remember that the approach and break away may vary in a hundred different ways, but in each attack you must, at a normal range, fly comparatively straight and hold your pip on the target long enough to do the job you started on. For that short

moment in any attack, you might as well forget flak and everything and concentrate on sighting; otherwise there is no point in carrying a lot of heavy .50 cal. slugs around in your guns all the time.

William B. Bailey, *P-47 pilot, 353rd Fighter Group*

The first few times a new pilot goes down on a ground target he is probably just plain scared. He feels there are hundreds of hidden guns which will open up on him at any moment. Naturally, this mental attitude will reflect on the firing accuracy of the individual concerned. He will invariably come in too fast, too high, or too low, slipping and skidding without much thought of hitting the target until he is closing so

Strafing run! Gun camera film from a 78th Fighter Group Mustang records part of the biggest day's bag by an Eighth AF fighter group during the war—125 German aircraft were claimed destroyed, nine by group CO John Landers, on 16 April 1945 on airfields in Czecho- slovakia. Total Eighth Air Force claims were an incredible 752 air- craft. The He 111 in the foreground is already burning smartly as .50 caliber hits register on and around the next German aircraft.

155

fast he has only the briefest interval to fire.

The first step in overcoming these errors is to instill in the pilot a sense of security. This is done by proper briefing, giving him an accurate knowledge of the existing flak installations, making arrangements for flak spotters, whose job it is to neutralize the flak, and to assign adequate top cover for the operation.

Wayne K. Blickenstaff, *P-47 pilot, 353rd Fighter Group*
Train busting is a great sport.

Joe L. Mason, *P-51 pilot, CO, 352nd Fighter Group*
On trains and convoys where you encounter no return fire, you must make every bullet count. Our ammunition is belted with five rounds of tracer fifty rounds from the end of the belt. We have a rule that you will not shoot past that tracer on a ground target—we lost some 109s one day because not a damn soul in the group had any bullets left. And good shooting is good shooting regardless of the target, and good shooting is what kills Germans.

On specific assigned targets I think bombing with fighters is O.K. I'm partial to dive bombing, as I think it's as accurate as any. Anything less than 1,000 pounds is not too much good on bridges. On all bridges we've bombed, we have only been successful in dropping one span. I'm sorry to have to admit it, but it seems to be the truth. Bombing with a fighter aircraft is one hundred percent personal skill, and it's just like playing basketball—the more you practice, the more baskets you can sink. We in the VIII Fighter Command have not had the

156

time, ranges, or equipment to practice fighter bombing to even approach the degree which could be obtained. But we are basically an escort outfit, and, in that, we have had sufficient practice to come closer to perfection. The score board shows that. You can mess up a lot of railroad by flying straight and level and dropping one bomb at a time. If done right, one group can break the tracks every ¼ mile for about fifty miles. That should drive the Hun nuts trying to fix it; it's not a permanent injury, but it makes him mad as hell. A good fighter-bomber pilot can hit his target from any dive angle at any altitude; that is what takes practice.

A fighter pilot who doesn't want to shoot his guns is no fighter pilot. I continuously have to warn them about non-military targets; the angle they shoot so it won't kill half the French in France, etc.

Shooting up convoys, and especially staff cars and dispatch riders, is considered great sport.

Avelin P. Tacon, Jr., *P-51 pilot, CO, 359th Fighter Group*
It is impossible to attack ground targets without having to pull up as the nose of the Mustang rides pretty well down at high speed. If the nose isn't far enough down, you can use 10 degrees of flaps, which is permissible up to 400 mph. This will bring your guns down on the ground right in front of you.

As for bombing, we much prefer dive bombing. Skip bombing is something we are not at all enthusiastic about. Probably because we can't hit a damn thing that way. The only thing we consider a skip bomb target is a tunnel mouth. All of

the bridges we have skip bombed have had low river banks and our bombs have just tumbled cross-country for about a mile before exploding.

Dive bombing is something else. We've gotten pretty accurate with dive bombing since we've had the Mustangs. By starting our dive from about 8,000 feet and releasing about 4,000 feet, we can get pretty good results. Particularly on bridge approaches and marshalling yards. Flak doesn't bother us much dive bombing, as we have plenty of speed. We like to dive bomb individually if there isn't any heavy flak bothering us.

As to the danger—everyone agrees that in strafing you're bound to get it in the end if you do enough of it, but that by being smart and taking every advantage, you can prolong it somewhat.

John B. Henry, Jr., *P-51 pilot, 339th Fighter Group*
Because of the extreme vulnerability of the P-51 airplane to any kind of damage, it is considered by most of our pilots that attacks on ground targets are not worth the risk unless those targets are poorly defended and are extremely vulnerable to .50 caliber fire.

After a long lull, when no opposition has been encountered from the Luftwaffe in the air, a couple of missions of ground strafing, despite the risk, does a lot for the morale of the pilots. Just to fire their guns and to know they are doing some damage boosts their spirits and tides them over until the next batch of Jerries comes to meet us in the air.

Incidentally, most of our airplanes have only four guns and usually at least one or two of them are jammed and useless. One of our "pet peeves" against this airplane is its lack of fire power in combat models prior to the "D" series.

Henry W. Brown, *P-47 pilot, 355th Fighter Group*

We had been escorting some bombers part of the way to Berlin. We were on our way home when I saw this airfield. There were four Junkers 88s parked in a line, with a lot more strung out around the field. I called them in on my radio. I was plenty green, but I sure wanted to shoot at some swastikas.

We didn't know much about ground strafing; no one in the outfit had ever done it. We got down real low, from about five miles out, and we gave it full throttle. We hopped over trees and buildings, going like hell, and we missed the field. We had to make a sharp left turn, all five of us. That screwed us up. Instead of being the second in line, I became the fourth.

The first guy blew up a Ju 88 right away. We still were real low.

The second guy opened up on the next Ju 88 in line. It began to burn just as he went over it. I thought he was going to crash into it. His tail did scrape the top of it. He was too close to fire at the third one, so he took the fourth. He shot the hell out of it, but it didn't burn—not right away.

I took the third one. It blew up. Just like that; real quick. I flew through the smoke of the first one to get to it. It was like going through a tunnel. Then I kicked the rudder and squirted at one that was parked to one

Just about everything you could hang on a fighter in 1944—metal drop tanks, 500-pound bombs and .50 caliber bullets. *USAF/NASM*

A Thunderbolt is loaded for a ground attack mission over France in support of advancing Allied armies. S/Sgt. Robert E. Robinson rearms the four .50s in the left wing as M/Sgt. James H. McGee and Sgt. John A. Koval move a 500 pound bomb onto the wing shackle. *USAF/NASM*

side. The flame shot out of it like water from a hose, out of its right side, and then [came] the biggest puff of black smoke I'd ever seen.

The flak was there the very first time. The minute we started at the field, they opened up on us. I knew that was bad, but I hadn't done any strafing before, so I really didn't know how bad that was. When they're firing at you right away, one attack is always enough. The odds get higher and higher every time.

But we made another attack. That was the roughest I've ever seen. Tracers and explosive cannon shells were popping all around us, like a rain of golf balls. We got some more planes, but it was like juggling a dozen ice picks, trying to shoot at the planes, and trying to shoot at the gun emplacements, going through all the smoke, trying to keep from crashing into something, moving as fast as we could. . . .

We didn't see the first boy after we started our second pass. I guess we left him there, somewhere. So there were three of us.

Two of us pulled away after that second pass. That had been murder. But the third guy was too excited to realize that his radio had been shot

The bomb dump, not a place for the weak-hearted. No wonder it was covered with camouflage netting. *USAF/NASM*

Capt. Dick Perley in front of the 313th Fighter Squadron operations tent at Toul-Ochey, near Nancy, France, before a mission. *Richard H. Perley*

out, and he didn't know he was making a third attack by himself. But he did [make the attack].

Every gun on that field was concentrated on him. Somehow he got through. He climbed up and joined us, and we started home. Then I saw another airfield with a couple of planes on it. I tore across it real fast, and set one on fire and kept right on going. I looked back—and damned if this third guy hadn't followed me!

He was climbing up to rejoin us again when the flak went after him once more. This time he really caught hell. One burst exploded right under his tail. Just as he called and told me he had been hit, another burst put some shrapnel through the rear of his cockpit canopy. Pieces hit him in the back of the head, in five different places, but he was a hard-headed boy. It just stunned him for a couple of seconds.

The other guy and I talked him back to England, telling him he'd

make it okay, and wondering to ourselves what was keeping his plane in the air. But he made it. He ground-looped when he landed, but he got out of the plane and was sitting on the grass when the ambulance got to him.

That plane . . . you had to see it to believe it. I don't think there was three feet of it that didn't have a hole in it, and the gas tank was bone dry.

They picked the shrapnel out of the guy's head, and the next morning he was on the flight line again, wrestling with everybody!

Claiborne H. Kinnard, Jr., *P–51 pilot, CO, 355th Fighter Group*

Boy, it was better than any movie ever made. Just before we met the bombers, south of the target, fourteen Messerschmitt 109s came streaming along. I wanted to hold the group as intact as possible so we could do the most damage to Ober-whatchacallit, so I told Jonesy to take them. He and his boys knocked down five, got two

probables, and damaged one. The rest of the Jerries got out of there. Jonesy and his squadron rejoined us near the target.

We took the Libs across and went down with the bombs. I streamed across the field once, at about 6,000 feet, to look it over good, and spot the gun emplacements. On the way I planned my runs. Boy, I'm telling you; things looked too good to be true! All the south and east side was literally covered with airplanes, like sitting ducks!

A big wall of smoke was rolling up from the hangars, and we used that to screen our approach. Soon as we busted through it, we started shooting. One twin-engined job blazed up in front of me right away.

We got to work in earnest. I looked behind me once, and boy, what a sight! I saw two German planes blow up; there was smoke and fire all over; guys pulling up firing, dodging each other, some going up, some

Lt. Robert C. Bucholz was killed in action in this 4th Fighter Group Mustang, *Suzy*, on 9 April 1945 when the group was strafing Munich-Brunnthal airdrome in Germany. Hit by flak, the P–51 went in before he had a chance to bail out. *Mark H. Brown/USAFA*

159

Maj. Pierce W. "Mac" McKennon runs up his *Ridge Runner III* at Debden, April 1945. Though he was forced to bail out twice, as indicated by the small parachutes behind the razorback boar, Mac managed to return to the 4th Fighter Group each time and get back on flying status. Crew chief Joseph B. Sills was constantly amazed at his pilot's energy and aggressiveness. *Joseph B. Sills*

diving, and all that smoke and fire. It was the damnedest thing I've ever seen. But there were a couple of surprises coming up.

I circled the field about the fourth attack, and passed over two batteries of heavy guns. It was that high altitude stuff. I couldn't help but grin, because I could see the gunners just standing there, their heads turned toward the field, with guns too big to use on us. They couldn't depress them enough to hit us.

I started to circle once more, and all hell broke loose on the field. I looked up and saw a little formation of our bombers going right over us, all but one. He had a wing gone, and was spinning down. I thought I'd lost my mind. I reckon they had gotten lost from the main bunch. Luckily, no one was hit badly.

We worked a little longer, and then the Jerries stopped vibrating and came out of their holes. They started pouring flak at us like water out of a firehose. We were about out of ammunition, and the place looked like a junkyard anyway, so we started home.

On the way out, seven Focke-Wulf 190s jumped out of the clouds behind us and started looking mean. I only had four ships with me. The group had split up. We turned suddenly and charged toward them, trying to look just as mean, or meaner. They ran. It was a good thing; I don't know what the hell we'd have done if they hadn't left. We didn't have any ammunition.

You know, I sure was proud of those boys. It may take time, but you can't keep those kids from winning. I don't know exactly what it is—but they've got it. Four of 'em were

starting across that field when those late bombers started unloading on it. One of 'em got a six inch hole in his wing from a bomb fragment, but they kept right on attacking and came around for more. One even thought that delayed action bombs were going off—but he kept right on going anyway. Maybe that's the answer. Nothing can stop them. They just keep right on going.

Jack Monaghan, *maintenance supply, 55th Fighter Group*

After all the long-range escort work we had been doing, the pilots became accustomed to carrying belly-tanks of fuel. As the war moved farther and farther into France and Germany, the fighters would go off carrying bombs for ground support instead of wing tanks with fuel. Some of the pilots would forget that because they had become accustomed to switching to wing-tanks as soon as they were off the ground. Unfortunately bombs on the wings don't carry fuel and they would go straight in. I don't know how many fighters we lost that way. It was pretty grim watching them pulling into the air and then suddenly see them wheeling down wing over wing to crash and burn. A couple of times when we finally reached the plane, we found the pilot standing there watching it burn.

Philip Savides, *P-47 pilot, 50th Fighter Group*

In the spring of 1945 I led a flight and dove down alone to strafe a retreating German convoy. While at low level, just as I was exulting in the find we had (it was a long, important looking string of trucks), I saw what

looked like red-hot golf balls arcing through the air, saw a field full of undisguised light antiaircraft guns, and in a second felt a couple of explosions.

I don't know what I hollered over the radio, but I attempted to let the guys know that I didn't expect anyone to join me. My right wing was showing flame from the cockpit out about half the length of the wing and the engine was pouring black smoke against the windscreen. Clearly the engine was not putting out power as it should and I prepared to get out of what appeared to be a doomed Thunderbolt.

I let go of the canopy, threw out my maps (didn't they always do that in the Hollywood movies?) and tore off and threw overboard my helmet, oxygen mask and earphones. In spite of the flame streaming back eight or ten feet from the trailing edge of the right wing, that was the side I decided to jump out of. With harness off and my hair flying in the smoke, I suddenly realized that the wing fire had stopped and it dawned on me that the engine was still running and the controls were intact. Besides, who would want to bail out in the area where you've just strafed?

If I could just put a few miles between me and that column of trucks before I had to parachute.... The engine sounded odd and continued to pour dense black smoke against the windshield and I had the impression that the power plant would soon quit altogether or catch on fire. Increased throttle seemed to do little good in my struggle to gain altitude, but I found that the plane performed better when I manually increased the rpm. Before long I had gained a few hundred feet and with the better perspective began

161

to look for a flat spot to make my belly landing. It would be tough to bring it down because the engine continued to belch dark oil smoke which condensed on the windscreen, making it impossible to see straight ahead.

A check of the instruments revealed that I had zero hydraulic pressure, but every thing else read OK. What really had me on edge, though, was that smoking engine. How long could it pump oil overboard like that without either running dry or starting a fire? Obviously the Germans had poked a hole in one of the front cylinder banks and with each stroke of the piston, my lubricant was spurting out of the damaged cylinder and being driven back by the air stream to sizzle into smoke as it struck the adjacent cylinders.

Although the film of oil kept creeping up on my windshield, obscuring my forward vision, I began to feel pretty comfortable. If the engine should seize from lack of oil, I could make a belly landing and if the vapor should flame, I had enough altitude to roll her over and drop out in my chute.

My wingman gave me the once over and helped with the heading toward home, but we couldn't talk because I had tossed away my helmet. I was unable to reach the spare headset which was supposed to be stowed under the seat. That flight continued to progress in my favor. At the moment I was first hit, I thought the only salvation was a low-level parachute jump into the hands of bitter enemies. Then perhaps we could get away a little to a bit of flat land in enemy territory for a belly landing.

Next—oh, you magnificent engine!—we made it to friendly territory and finally there is the field. My wingman called the tower for clearance to land straight in and the controller responded that he couldn't yet see the planes, but he did have my smoke in sight!

I had been pampering the power for 45 minutes since I was hit and never did believe it would turn for more than another minute, so I resolved that I would land on the first pass and avoid the strain of another climb. Reasoning that I had no hydraulic fluid and that I was shot up in the area of the landing gear, I decided to land wheels up beside the runway on the right. I cut the power and as I neared the field I began to realize I was too high and too hot. How ironic—after 45 minutes of praying that the aircraft would fly fast and high, I now wanted to slow down and drop.

I was over the end of the runway with about 100 feet and 150 mph. When I saw only half of the runway remained ahead of me, I eased the stick forward and flew the plane

The 50th Fighter Group's Thunderbolts dispersed across the forward operating field near Nancy, France. *Richard H. Perley*

into the dirt at about 150 mph. Thunderbolts with the gear up are inclined to land a little longer than those whose wheels are down! The deceleration forced my body forward with my head tipped forward as if I were trying to look at my knees. (The next morning, when dressing, I noticed I had a pink stripe in front of each shoulder where I been thrown against the shoulder harness.)

As the plane stopped, I got out so fast I don't remember undoing the harness and I believe the plane was rocking back toward the tail as I ran straight off the right wing tip (why the right side?). The ambulance guys drove up and were looking in the cockpit when I turned around and walked back to the plane. When I got there, one of them asked me where

Lt. Dick Perley leans against the only contraption conceived by man that could overcome "General Mud," the mighty Cletrac, at Toul-Ochey airfield near Nancy, France, winter 1944–45. Like other Ninth Air Force fighter groups, the 50th operated, for the most part, from unprepared areas covered by pierced steel planking (PSP), living in tents and trying to find enough heat. *Richard H. Perley*

the pilot was. I had left there so quickly that he hadn't even seen me as they were driving toward the spot. The prop blades were each neatly and uniformly bent backwards around the engine.

Gilbert C. Burns, Jr., *P–47 pilot, 50th Fighter Group*

My fifth combat mission changed my viewpoint on combat flying in many ways. The first four missions I had flown mechanically. The hands and feet flew the plane, the finger squeezed the trigger, doing automatically all the things I had been taught. But this mission got me thinking.

I thought about *killing.*

I had killed the rear gunner in an Me 110 by rote. Very nonchalantly, like brushing my teeth. However, when I killed three flak gunners, I was mentally and acutely aware of just what had occurred. I had seen their bodies being blown apart and was keenly concerned that I had done something serious. I had a mental reaction.

I thought about being *wounded.*

I heard a pilot say on radio after he had pulled up from the airfield that he was hit in the knee and that he could not stop the blood from flowing. He wanted to bail out and hoped he could find a German doctor. From that day onward, during every mission, I wore four loose tourniquets around my upper arms and thighs. I thought that if I was hit I could just take up on the tourniquets, as they were already in place.

I thought about being *captured.*

The stories we had heard were not pretty. The civilians in Germany understandably hated us for bombing and strafing their towns and unintentionally killing many of their own. We had heard rumors of our captured fliers being tied to horses' tails by the ankles, dragged through the streets and stoned and beaten by the civilians. True or not, these stories now prompted me to further protect myself in case of a bail out.

My Colt .45 automatic pistol was my first concern. I set up some bottles as targets 50 feet away and began firing practice. Not one bottle could I hit. I tried at 25 feet with the same bad results. When at 10 feet I was not good, I put the .45 in my barracks bag and forgot about it. I managed to obtain a .38 Colt long barrel six shooter with an 8 inch barrel. A minimum of practice showed that with this weapon I was quite good and so carried it on my hip on the rest of my missions. I would have preferred carrying a Luger. If I did bail out and was evading and ran out of ammunition, cartridges for the Luger would be easier to come by. I found out years later that all the local German police carried Lugers. But at Toul, France, a Luger was not available.

Also at that time the German High Command learned that American pilots were carrying .45s. They were quite concerned about this, with visions of a flier descending in his parachute, blasting away with his .45. What they did not know was that nine out of ten pilots couldn't hit the broad side of a barn with it. They had nothing to fear about the Colt .45.

Chapter 10

Photo Recon

Ralph P. Willett, *F-5 crew chief, 3rd Photo Group*

The ground haze that was lifting from the field under the weak rays of winter sun uncovered a bee-hive of activity on the line of this forward aerodrome. Mechanics in greasy coveralls swarmed around the sleek lines of the photo plane; a lumbering, red-flagged gasoline truck scurried up and deposited its fuel. Camera technicians inserted the film magazines and set shutter speeds and lens openings. The crew chief nonchalantly climbed up to the pilot's housing and abstractly began polishing the canopy of the cockpit, all the while keeping a sharp watch on the activities about him.

Everything was set now, but he continued polishing the smooth lucite in even, round, unhurried motions, keeping the rhythm set by his jaws. At last the pilot, a small young fellow, half the age of the crew chief, drove up; even his padded flying clothes did not obliterate the impression of extreme youth. Quickly he climbed to

the wing of the plane, silently accepted the mechanic's aid in settling himself in his cockpit and quickly became engrossed in the manipulation of the myriad of switches and dials in front of him. The previously tested engines turned over quickly with a start, coughed once or twice, and settled down to a deep throttle roar that spoke of unbridled power.

Throwing up clouds of dust, the plane taxied out to the runway and soon was hurtling into space. Unfettered now, the plane began making great circles, climbing, always climbing, until it became an unbelievably small speck against the blue-gray winter sky. The crew chief, jaws still working unhurriedly, cloth clutched in his closed fist, followed the plane until it abruptly swung north and was lost from view and then turned and walked away.

No, there is no full blown action at a photo recon base, but there is drama. The drama of an individual pitted alone against unknown opposition, of machines and men

working as one organ, of callousness born of necessity; there is the drama of accomplishment; of several hundred men working with dogged insistency, impersonally and yet with the human element, laughing at their own situation when it could become no worse; of C-rations, seas of mud, cold tents without cots, goldbricks and eager-beavers, religious services and poker games.

John Blyth, *Spitfire pilot, 7th Photo Group*

When I heard that we were getting enough Spitfires to equip one squadron, I asked to be transferred. I had dreamed since high school of flying a Spitfire and now it was becoming a reality. My first mission in the Spitfire Mark XI was in April 1944. I went in at 36,000 ft. and was thrilled by the Spit's performance. It exceeded my expectations because it was so much more than the Mark V I had flown locally. The 1,650 hp Rolls-Royce Merlin really made a difference. I loved its response at

A well-worn F–5A Lightning in synthetic haze paint, with cameras instead of guns in the nose. *Fred Bamberger via David W. Menard*

This recce Lightning has a uniform blue haze color scheme which was applied over a black lacquer base coat. The "Photo Joes" wanted to blend in with their environment as much as possible. *National Archives via Dana Bell*

altitude and didn't mind that it only had one engine.

I don't know about other pilots, but to me the English Channel was like an invisible wall. At some point one passed from being relatively safe to entering the unknown. Mentally, each of us probably handled it differently, but flying alone and unarmed was quite different than flying with others. Actually, I was usually busy climbing on course and navigating while crossing the channel and tried not to think about it. Oftentimes part of the mission would be on instruments making navigation more difficult. We often had several targets to photograph, making at least three runs over each, all the while watching for German fighters or our own fighters that figured a Spitfire in this deep must have been captured.

On the way home, it was almost guaranteed that we would face a headwind. Sometimes it seemed forever to reach the English Channel. If I was low on fuel, I would land at RAF Bradwell Bay or RAF Manston stations to refuel and make a bathroom stop. A cramped cockpit at -50 degrees is not the most comfortable work place. At altitude, the heater in the Spitfire or F-5 wasn't much good.

From April 1944 to October I flew 36 missions in the Spitfire. The F-5 had been limited for a period to shorter missions because of problems. It became the mission of the Spits to fly the deeper penetrations and subsequently, I flew missions to Berlin, Munich and eastern and central areas of Germany. Most of these were at 30,000 ft. or above. If the contrails were at 22,000 ft. (winter) I would go to 36,000 or 38,000. In the summertime, I would usually hit contrails and then drop to around 30,000 ft. The buzz bomb sites on the coast of France were flown at 15,000 ft.

All of my missions were unarmed and without fighter escort. Robert R. Smith and Waldo Bruns failed to return from a mission to the Polish border. Glenn Wiebe was then sent in and he failed to return. It was then decided to send in Spitfires. Three of us were to go in at thirty minute intervals. Walt Simon was to go to the synthetic oil refinery at Brux, Czechoslovakia. I was next going to Ruhland synthetic oil refinery (Polish border) and Kermit Bliss would be behind me. We refueled at RAF Manston for maximum fuel. I was at 30,000 ft. on the way in and could hear the German radar pick me up. I could hear it build up and fade on my headset. Being in the middle, I figured they would intercept Walt first. My thoughts were of the three that hadn't come back and what might have happened to them. Also, Glenn Wiebe and I had started first grade together in Dallas, Oregon, and what a coincidence it might be if the Germans also got me.

Near Dresden I saw a factory that had been bombed and figured I would make a pass across it and save someone a trip. It probably saved my life! As I rolled into a turn to align the target and turned on my cameras, I noticed an aircraft diving and closing rapidly on my tail. He must have been above me and I missed him. At first I thought it was a jet because of the black exhaust trail. It was an Me 109 with a yellow prop spinner and yellow and orange checkered nose. There might have been others. In a Spit, the throttle was full forward at altitude so I pushed full forward on the propeller control to pick up speed. I flew straight and level and played like I didn't see him. He probably figured he had another victory for the Fatherland and was about to squeeze the trigger when I pulled back abruptly on the stick. Then and there we must have parted company. When I rolled into a turn and looked down, he was underneath me. The climb at that altitude surprised me. Any other evasive maneuver and he probably would have nailed me. I then remembered my cameras and turned them off.

For a short time I didn't know my location. I ended up over Brux, which was on fire, and took pictures, went on to Ruhland, both my other targets and returned to Manston with only several gallons of fuel remaining. I was put in for the DFC but was turned down. The 7th PRG had to be the most poorly decorated unit in the 8th Air Force.

Dan Burrows, *F-5 pilot, 7th Photo Group*

On 20 April 1944, I was operations officer of the 22nd Squadron, and recall that the spring weather was good over England and Europe. Good enough to complete a mission and Doc [Malcolm D. Hughes] was planning to announce his return to Mount Farm by improving the low fly-by over the Intelligence building after his first ops flight exactly ten months earlier.

George Nesselrode and I learned of this from his crew chief and had been monitoring his position with the tower and Base Ops. We positioned ourselves at a vantage point in front of the Intelligence briefing building, having first discussed jumping in a jeep and driving out to mid-field, but thought better of it—too inviting a target. Looking to the southwest we saw the silhouette of the F-5 banking down over the far perimeter, level out and then *disappear!* We knew the field had a rise in the center, but up until then, never realized you could hide behind it. We knew then that Doc was serious, and as he popped into view cutting grass at a high rate of speed, it was obvious he was heading straight for us, and it would not be prudent to remain in the line of flight.

George let out a whoop, threw his hat in the air, and we departed rapidly at a ninety degree angle. It couldn't have been more than two seconds when I heard what sounded like 20 mm cannon fire—glancing over my left shoulder I saw the F-5 tail booms disappear over the back of the building. Knowing that the maintenance hangar was just a short distance behind, we braced for the crash and explosion. Instead we saw the plane pulling up into a climbing left turn, heading back toward the runway, but making a strange ffft-fft-fft sound.

By then George and I had stopped, marveling at the seeming miracle, when something equally astonishing occurred. The door to the Intelligence building flew open and a ghost appeared, a fearful apparition all in white, waving its arms, making strange sounds and surrounded by what seemed a cloud of mist. George and I stood with our mouths open, until we slowly recognized the earthly form of "Pappy" Lytton Doolittle, the patriarchal Intelligence Officer of the 13th Photo Squadron. It was subsequently found that he was covered with plaster dust, and he and Capt. Walt Hickey, 27th Photo Intelligence Officer, thought they'd been hit by a V bomb, but only Pappy suffered a slight cut on the forehead.

By now, troops who had been witnessing the show started showing up, wondering what had happened, and we had brushed Pappy off and explained the situation. He mentioned something about [being] eligible for a Purple Heart. We realized that Doc had landed, and watched as he taxied toward the Ops ramp, with *one prop feathered*, no simple feat in itself.

Nesselrode and I ran over as Doc braked to a stop, opened the canopy, stepped out on the wing and said, "Let's see you bastards beat *that* one!"

A 3rd Photo Group F-5A Lightning comes in to land in Italy, 1944. The synthetic haze blue paint was designed to make the recce aircraft basically invisible until very close range. The color blended in quite well at high altitude. On solo flights, without armament, it was important that they avoid enemy fighters. *Peter M. Bowers via Dana Bell*

The need for accurate weather reporting over the Continent resulted in the formation of the 25th Bomb Group (Recon), which flew fast de Havilland Mosquito Mk. XVIs from April 1944 to the end of the war. The 25th's Mosquitos flew out in advance of bomber formations to report weather and target strikes but also to take photos and fly chaff screening missions for the bombers. This Mossie was attached to the Group's 653rd Bomb Squadron. *Edward R. Richie*

Doc told me later that as he started his pull up to go over the Intelligence building, he mushed slightly—just enough so that one prop struck the flat roof, pulling him down. Of course, this required desperate action, since he was looking straight at the 381st hangar, so he hauled back on the wheel, at the same time noticing severe vibration. He knew if he didn't do something quickly, he would literally lose an engine. Everything was shaking so badly that the instruments were unreadable. Taking a deep breath, he reached to the left and feathered a prop. Fortunately, he made the correct selection—the rest, for him, was a piece of cake. . . .

The briefing room [was] in a shambles, plaster and white dust everywhere, with neon lights hanging by one chain, the other end resting on the table. There were three gashes in the ceiling, where, amazingly, the prop had not hit any of the large support beams and it was obvious that the blade tips had to have been a few inches inside the room. . . .

The Group Commander, George Lawson, told me, "I rushed over to survey the damage, and immediately instructed the engineers to start repair on the gashes in the roof. Speed was essential if Doc's latest antic was to be suppressed. Of course, something of this magnitude was not about to be kept quiet and soon enough Wing Headquarters had people at Mount Farm making noises about 'court martial, loss of wings and other nasty punitive measures.' My rebuttal was 'why ground a talented pilot, when we need him here to fight the war and not stuck in some office back in the boondocks?' Since our losses were running about 33% and we needed pilots, the argument stood up."

My recollection is that he was grounded for 30 days and afterward contributed to the war effort until the spring of 1945. . . . Doc was lucky in more ways than one—when it comes right down to it, Wing could have got him for breaking and entering!

German divisional order, 1944

Enemy aerial photo reconnaissance detects our every movement, every concentration, every weapon, and immediately after detection, every one of these objectives is smashed.

An F-6C Mustang of the 15th Tactical Reconnaissance Squadron on the European continent in late 1944. Most tac recon outfits had Malcolm Hoods fitted to their razorback F-6s for better visibility. The camera port in the rear plexiglass panel is just visible, along with at least four kill markings. Flown primarily at low level, tactical reconnaissance was hazardous but thrilling and because the recce version of the Mustang retained its guns, self-defense resulted in numerous kills. *Ralph Woolner via Monogram Aviation Publications*

An F–5 Lightning of the 3rd Photo Group on short final to its base in
Italy. *Peter M. Bowers*

An F–5 Lightning climbing for altitude. *Lockheed*

Chapter 11

Ruptured Duck

Herbert R. Rutland, Jr., *P-51 pilot, 356th Fighter Group*

When the war ended in Europe, my fighter group in England was disbanded, and I found myself in Germany with the occupation forces. We were engaged in moving troops back and forth in transport planes operating out of a remote airfield near the town of Illesheim, [then I was] transferred to R-29, the airfield at Herzogenaurach.

As flying had been curtailed, pilots had to wait their turn to get an occasional flight. In the meantime, some turned up with motorcycles, delighting in roaring down the narrow roads in close formation at high speed. More than one ox-cart took to the ditch upon hearing the approach of the crazy Americans. After numerous complaints and a growing casualty list, the base commander called a halt to this pastime.

Monday was laundry day at the base. Arms bare to the elbows, the female DPs [displaced persons] would gather the woolen uniforms and scrub them in tubs of pure aviation gasoline. One day a loud explosion sounded from my barracks, and smoke filled the building. When the smoke cleared and it was determined that no serious injuries had been incurred, one of the DPs admitted to breaking the rules: she had moved the tub inside, out of the cold. We dubbed the cheerful, young Polish girl "Blockbuster"—the same name given by the British to their largest bomb.

The base was not without social activity, and periodically a gala was held at the non-commissioned officers' club. Young ladies from throughout the area were invited to attend. More often, the entire female population descended upon the base. The prospect of food, drink, and dancing lured many on foot over long distances. As they began their long trek home in the darkness, most could be seen holding morsels of leftovers or candy bars. If some of the ladies appeared more buxom than upon their arrival, it was likely that cigarette butts had been collected and stored in consideration of the smokers at home.

By the spring of 1946, the 354th Fighter Group [based at R-29] no longer existed as a fighting unit. Most of its members had returned home, and a large number of its P-51s had been systematically turned into scrap upon orders from above. German civilians hired to assist in the demolition had every reason to believe that the Americans were truly out of their minds: those of us who had flown and loved those beautiful machines watched in dismay as the explosive charges were placed and then set off. It was like a knife in the heart.

On May 1, 1946, I climbed into one of the remaining Mustangs and headed south for the Alps. As I cruised among the snowcapped peaks, I found myself, by habit, searching the sky behind me for little specks that might be unfriendly planes. Touching down back at "Herzo," I completed my last flight as a fighter pilot.

June 1945. The war in Europe is over and the Mustangs of the 55th Fighter Group are lined up for inspection at Wormingford. Slowly each fighter group in the AAF would drift back to peacetime status, men would go home, units would be transferred or disbanded and the massive number of aircraft would be scrapped. *Robert T. Sand*

As GIs roamed Germany they came across numerous yards of wrecked or scrapped Luftwaffe aircraft. This dump at Kaufbeuren airfield, Bavaria, contained quite an assortment of machines that were shot up or sabotaged by retreating Germans, and 55th Fighter Group mechanics found it fascinating to compare the aircraft with what they had been working on. Bob Sand recalls, "The line chiefs took to these shattered planes, patched some up and got them running. The enlisted men had been promised flying lessons in American light observation planes, which never materialized, so some of the men were hot to fly their resurrected planes, but probably wisely, were given thumbs down. However, they were given permission to taxi them when the field wasn't busy. I'll never forget one pretty powerful twin engine plane. The guy would get at one end of the runway, rev the engines high, lift off the brakes and go roaring down the runway, then brake so he could stop at the end of the runway and start the opposite way. As a long frustrated flyer, how I commiserated with that man. Still, it was a pleasure to look down on these planes after looking up at them so often in England." *Robert T. Sand*

173

As the months of occupation wore on in Germany, groups were decommissioned and aircraft slowly stripped to keep others flying. The derelicts, such as *Pard* of the 359th Fighter Group sitting on a field in Germany, were painful viewing for pilots and ground crews as they watched their once-vital birds get plucked. When personnel were released from active duty and sent home on accumulated service points, they were entitled to sew a small eagle and wreath within a diamond emblem on the sleeves of their uniforms. This quickly became known as a "ruptured duck." symbolizing both men and machines as they were discarded from what used to be the world's mightiest air force. *Fagen via Dave Menard*

Happy Warrior, a Ninth Air Force P–47D, has been put out to pasture in Germany. National, unit and personal markings have been painted over. *Fagen via Dave Menard*

On this page and following page
The sad end of the once-proud 354th Fighter Group's Mustangs at Herzogenaurach, Germany. Germans were hired to chop the P-51s down, then burn them—a task they would have given anything for the chance to do just months before. It puzzled them even more than the Americans who were left to watch. *Herbert R. Rutland, Jr.*

176